KNOWING THE SON

Colin Dye

Sovereign World

Sovereign World Ltd
PO Box 777
Tonbridge
Kent TN11 0ZS
England

Scriptural quotations are from the New King James Version, Thomas Nelson Inc., 1991.

ISBN 1 85240 209 1

Typeset by CRB Associates, Reepham, Norfolk
Printed in England by Clays Ltd, St Ives plc.

FOREWORD

The material in this *Sword of the Spirit* series has been developed over the past ten years at Kensington Temple in London as we have sought to train leaders for the hundreds of churches and groups we have established. Much of the material was initially prepared for the students who attend the International Bible Institute of London – which is based at our church.

Over the years, other churches and colleges have asked if they may use some of our material to help them establish training courses for leaders in their towns and countries. This series has been put together partly to meet this growing need, as churches everywhere seek to train large numbers of new leaders to serve the growth that God is giving.

The material has been constantly refined – by myself, by the students as they have responded, by my many associate pastors, and by the staff at the Bible Institute. In particular, my colleague Timothy Pain has been responsible for sharpening, developing and shaping my different courses and notes into this coherent series.

I hope that many people will use this series in association with our developing Satellite Bible School, but I also pray that churches around the world will use the books to train leaders.

We live at a time when increasing numbers of new churches are being started, and I am sure that we will see even more startling growth in the next few decades. It is vital that we re-examine the way we train and release leaders so that these new churches have the best possible biblical foundation. This series is our contribution to equipping tomorrow's leaders with the eternal truths that they need.

Colin Dye

CONTENTS

INTRODUCTION

The twelve books in this *Sword of the Spirit* series have been constructed both to 'stand alone' as individual guide-books about particular biblical topics *and* to 'join together' to form a cohesive and thorough course which will establish you in ministry and equip you to teach others to know God and his purposes more deeply.

All twelve books refer to each other and are fundamentally inter-related, so you need to study them all if you want to grasp the full picture of 'the Word and the Spirit'. Each of the books, however, is a full-and-complete unit for study – except, perhaps, this one.

Jesus of Nazareth, the Christ, the Lord, the Saviour, the Son of the living God, so dominates the Scriptures that it is impossible to describe the fullness of his nature and work in such a slim volume.

In one sense, all twelve books in this series are about the Son – who is himself the Word of God. For example, we study his holy teaching in *The Rule of God*, his prayer life in *Effective Prayer*, his earthly service in *Ministry in the Spirit*, his evangelistic mission in *Reaching the Lost*, his trinitarian interdependence in *Knowing the Father*, and so on. Although we touch on each of these aspects of the Son's life in this book, you will need to study them in more depth in the other books.

Most importantly, we deal with the great abiding purpose of the Son in *Salvation by Grace*; it is imperative, therefore, that you study *Knowing the Son* in conjunction with *Salvation by Grace*. You will not grasp the fullness of the Son's mission without studying both books.

In this book, we are more concerned with knowing 'who the Son is' than with knowing 'what he has done' – we cover that elsewhere. We focus on the mystery of his fully divine, fully human nature; we consider the uniqueness of his being and the unique events of his life; we examine his working relationship with the Father and the Spirit; and we think about the cross in the way that it is presented by the Gospels.

This is a book for believers who are eager to study God's Word to learn how Jesus of Nazareth can be both one of the sons of a simple carpenter and the only Son of the Almighty Creator; it is a book for disciples whose minds are open to receive God's biblical revelation about the nature, mission, purpose and destiny of his beloved Son.

Please ensure that you read all the references – and tick the margin boxes as you go along to show that you have. Answer every question and think through each point as it is made. Before moving on to a new section, think carefully about the implications of what you have studied. Please allow God to speak to you as you study his word.

At the end of the book, there is some activity material and questions. Please make sure that you study Parts 1–9 before beginning to work through the activities, as this will ensure that you have an overview of the biblical teaching about the Son before you try to apply the details of any one aspect. These questions will help you to grasp and apply the scriptural material that you have studied.

You will also be able to use the activity pages when you teach the material to small groups. Please feel free to photocopy these pages and distribute them to any group you are leading. Although you should work through all the questions when you are studying on your own, please don't expect a small group to cover all the material.

By the time you finish this book, it is my prayer that you will have a far better understanding of the wonderful person and work of our Lord and Saviour Jesus Christ – and, especially, of the way that his Sonship should shape our lives as sons and daughters of the one Father.

Even more than this, I pray that you will be inspired to greater devotion, and to more dedicated discipleship, by the submissive dependence of the Son – who willingly came in suffering and death (and will willingly come again soon in power and glory) to rescue humanity from evil and establish the kingdom of God.

Colin Dye

PART ONE

the fully human son

Throughout history, there have always been some people who think that Jesus is only divine, and others who believe that he is only human. All Christian traditions, however, despite any disagreements about other matters, have always been united in their understanding that Jesus is a unique being who is simultaneously both *fully human* and *fully divine*.

Most ordinary people find it easy to recognise that Jesus was fully a man, but they go on to assume that he was only a man: they find it hard to imagine that a human being could also be a divine being.

This popular false assumption is the main reason why many churches emphasise Jesus' divinity. But we misrepresent the Son whenever we focus more on one aspect of his being than on another; instead, we should concentrate equally on his full divinity *and* his full humanity.

Of course, the New Testament teaches that Jesus is much more than just another man; but it sets this teaching against the background of his genuine humanity. So too in this book, although we concentrate on *Knowing the Son* who is exalted in a great host of ways, we begin by establishing that he is fully human.

THE HUMANITY OF JESUS

The Gospels of Matthew, Mark and Luke present similar portraits of Jesus: they may use different material to offer distinctive emphases, but they are all concerned with the same person. (We consider some of the extra-biblical evidence for Jesus' human life in *Reaching the Lost*.)

Mark 1:1 ☐

In his opening verse, Mark suggests that he is introducing someone who is more than a man, yet he goes on to present a human picture of a suffering, serving Jesus. In contrast, Matthew and Luke begin with birth stories which record the humble beginnings of Jesus' life: they present him in an ordinary human home, subject to all the ordinary pressures that this involves.

Luke 2:39–52 ☐

Luke 2:39–52 is the only biblical account of Jesus' childhood, and this reveals something of the essential humanity of his earthly family. Luke's 'asides' in 2:40 and 2:51–52 suggest that Jesus developed to adulthood according to the normal laws of human growth.

All the Gospels present Jesus' baptism as the start of his ministry, and show how he identified with the ordinary people who were flocking to his cousin John. The subsequent temptations reveal that Jesus, like all other people, had to endure severe moral and physical testing.

Matthew, Mark and Luke present Jesus as a thoroughly first-century human. For example:

- *he inhabits a world of Pharisees, Sadducees and Herodians*

- *his short life span is typical of first-century Palestine*

- *he heals and teaches people who are facing the same social and political tensions that he faces*

- *he is a man among men who does what ordinary people do – eats meals in homes, travels by foot and boat, pays taxes and mixes with a great variety of people*

- *he is deeply compassionate towards the socially isolated*

- *he criticises hypocrisy and argues with religious leaders*

- *he is so distressed in Gethsemane that he sweats profusely*

- *he feels abandoned on the cross*

Yet, against this human backdrop, the three Gospels make it plain that Jesus was quite different from all other humans. For example, he:

- *claims authority to go beyond the law*

- *forgives sins*

- *commands nature*

- *casts out demons*

- *is transfigured before three of his disciples in a way which is impossible for other living persons*

- *uses and accepts titles which set him in a class of his own*

The Gospels continually present Jesus both as fully identified with humanity *and* as completely distinct from humanity – and they seem unaware of the tension that this creates for many readers.

John's Gospel

It is generally recognised that John's Gospel presents Jesus' divinity particularly clearly. In contrast to Matthew and Luke's human 'family trees', it begins with a heavenly genealogy which stresses his pre-existence and divine origin. Even so, John 1:14 emphasises that the Word became *flesh* and 'dwelt' or 'tabernacled' among us.

John 1:14 ☐

We consider John's presentation of the incarnation as 'God pitching his tent in humanity' in *Salvation by Grace*, and see this means that God manifested himself in real human flesh. Although this Gospel strongly underlines Jesus' divine nature, it often draws attention to the reality of his fully human 'tabernacle'. For example, John's Gospel shows that:

- *many people regard Jesus as a rabbi* – 1:38; 3:2; 9:2; 11:8

John 1:38 ☐
3:2 ☐
9:2 ☐
11:8 ☐

- *he is exhausted by a journey* – 4:6

4:6–7 ☐

- *he experiences thirst* – 4:7; 19:28

19:28 ☐

- *he arouses hatred* – 7:44; 10:31–39; 11:57

7:44 ☐
10:31–39 ☐
11:57 ☐

- *he weeps at the death of a friend* – 11:33–35

11:33–35 ☐

- *he washes feet* – 13:1–5

13:1–5 ☐

- *he prepares a meal* – 21:9

21:9 ☐

The early church

Although the book of Acts focuses on the exalted Christ, it often introduces him as 'Jesus of Nazareth' – for example, Acts 2:22; 3:6; 4:10; 6:14; 10:38; 22:8; 26:9. This shows that he was a real, historical person who lived as a genuine man in the small town of Nazareth.

Because Paul's letters contain few facts about Jesus, some scholars have suggested that he knew little about the historical Jesus. But Acts 9:26 records that Paul met the apostles in Jerusalem; Acts 12:25 describes Mark as Paul's companion; and Acts 23:35 and 24:23–27 show that Paul spent two years in the Praetorium at Caesarea (the Roman capital of Palestine) with freedom to meet other disciples. (Acts implies that Luke cared for Paul during this imprisonment, and it is very likely that Luke researched his Gospel during this two year period. If this is so, he would surely have discussed his findings with Paul.)

The truth is that Paul's epistles are letters of doctrinal instruction and pastoral correction to young churches: they do not attempt to portray Jesus' personality or teach about the events of his life. Even so, Paul's letters contain many details which underscore Jesus' historical humanity. For example, Paul shows that Jesus:

- *was descended from David* – Romans 1:3

- *belonged to Israel according to the flesh* – Romans 9:5

- *was sent by God at a specific time to be born of a woman and to live under the law* – Galatians 4:4

- *had a brother (whom Paul knew)* – Galatians 1:19

- *was poor* – 2 Corinthians 8:9

- *was crucified, buried and resurrected* – 1 Corinthians 15:4

- *instituted the Lord's Supper* – 1 Corinthians 11:23–26

- *was meek and gentle* – 2 Corinthians 10:1

- *was righteous and sinless* – Romans 5:18; 2 Corinthians 5:21

- *was humble and steadfast* – Philippians 2:6–8; 2 Thessalonians 3:5

- *was a man in the same way that Adam was a man* – Romans 5:12–21; 1 Corinthians 15:21–22

- *was a man* – 1 Timothy 2:5

The book of Hebrews begins, in 1:1–3, by introducing Jesus as the exalted Son of God, the heir of all things, the Creator of everything. But it then balances this by providing a great deal of information about the Son's fully human nature. Hebrews shows, for example, that Jesus:

- *was lower than the angels and concerned with people in his mission – 2:9, 16*

- *shared human flesh and blood like all people – 2:14*

- *was subject to temptation – 2:18; 4:15*

- *prayed with cries and tears – 5:7*

- *learned obedience through suffering – 2:10; 5:8–9*

- *experienced godly fear – 5:7*

- *regarded death as an inescapable part of his mission – 2:9, 14*

In *Salvation by Grace*, we see that Hebrews concentrates on the idea of Jesus' 'sacrificial' death. It establishes Jesus' qualifications as the great high priest of humankind, and shows that his humanity is indispensable to the idea of him offering himself as a sacrifice through the Spirit: we see this, for example, in 9:14, 26–28; 10:10, 20.

Quite simply, men and women would have no access to God if Jesus the human had not mediated with God and pioneered the way.

The whole New Testament keeps on making a double presentation of Jesus' *divine sonship* and his *perfect humanity*. It reveals him simultaneously both as the Son who reflects the glory of God and as the human who can be tempted as we are. This is an important truth, and we must work hard to keep both aspects close together in our understanding, our experience and our proclamation.

THE SINLESS HUMANITY OF JESUS

The New Testament does not only present Jesus as a fully human being, it also stresses that he is a sinless human being – in fact, that he is the only fully sinless person that there has been since Adam and Eve before their fall. We see this in Hebrews 4:15; 1 Peter 2:22; 1 John 3:5.

Hebrews 1:1–3 ☐
2:9 ☐
2:14–18 ☐
4:15 ☐
5:7–9 ☐

Hebrews 9:14 ☐
9:26–28 ☐
10:10 ☐
10:20 ☐

Hebrews 4:15 ☐
1 Peter 2:22 ☐
1 John 3:5 ☐

Although Jesus makes no specific claim to sinlessness in the Gospels, there are plenty of pointers towards his absolute perfection, and there is nothing which contradicts this idea. For example, Jesus:

- *never makes any confession of sin*

- *calls people to repentance without revealing any need for himself to repent*

- *submits to John's baptism 'to fulfil all righteousness', not to signify repentance* – Matthew 3:14–15

- *shows an acutely sensitive resistance to evil* – Matthew 16:23

- *fully resists temptation* – Matthew 4:1–11

- *condemns hypocrisy, without anyone responding by counter-condemning his hypocrisy* – Matthew 23:1–36

- *urges other people to be as perfect as God, without involving himself in the exhortation or attracting any suggestions that he is less than perfect* – Matthew 5:20

- *differentiates himself from his 'evil' hearers* – Matthew 7:11

- *is never accused of not living up to his own teaching*

- *makes astonishing claims which would be totally arrogant if his moral status did not match them* – John 8:12

- *is never accused of sin, even when he invites his listeners to charge him in this way* – John 8:44

- *claims to do the will of God in a way which suggests that it is unthinkable for him to do otherwise* – John 10:37; 14:10–11, 31; 15:10; 17:4

- *claims to be one with the Father* – John 10:30; 17:22

The early church often referred implicitly to Jesus' sinlessness by describing him as 'holy' and as 'righteous'. We see this, for example, in Acts 2:27; 3:14; 4:30; 7:52; 17:31.

The fact of Jesus' total sinlessness is clearest in Paul's teaching about salvation. Just as Hebrews shows that Jesus had to be fully human to act as the mediating high priest, so 2 Corinthians 5:21 and Galatians 3:13 show that Jesus had to be fully sinless for his death to be an acceptable and effective sacrifice. When we think carefully, it should be clear that Jesus could be made sin only if he was without sin, and that he could be made a curse only if he was not under a curse himself.

Over the years, some scholars have wondered whether Jesus' absolute sinlessness means that it was impossible for him to commit sin. The New Testament, however, asserts both that he was tested in every way that we are, *and* that he was completely sinless.

Other scholars have wondered whether Jesus could have been truly human without being predisposed to sin in the way that all humans are. But the New Testament never suggests that Jesus had to become identical with humanity in its fallen nature to redeem it from sin. Instead, it suggests that Jesus was another Adam – that he was truly human (as God intended and intends all humanity to be) but without the post-Eden fallen nature.

As Adam demonstrated, even perfect, unfallen humanity possessed the freedom to sin when faced with real temptation. The true wonder of Jesus' sinless humanity is that he alone has not succumbed to the temptation to say 'No' to God – and to this we owe our salvation.

THE SON

In *Knowing the Father*, we see that the Bible reveals many facets of God's nature through the names by which he introduces himself to his people, and through the names and titles with which people are inspired to address him.

It is the same with the fully human and fully divine aspects of the Son. The New Testament reveals that he is, for example:

- *Jesus* – Matthew 1:1

- *the Christ* – Matthew 1:1

- *the Son of David* – Matthew 1:1

- *the Son of Abraham* – Matthew 1:1

- *the King of the Jews* – Matthew 2:2

- *the Nazarene* – Matthew 2:23

Matthew 1:1 ☐
2:2 ☐
2:23 ☐

Matthew 3:3 ☐
3:17 ☐
4:3 ☐
4:7 ☐
8:19–20 ☐
9:15 ☐
12:8 ☐
16:16 ☐
21:11 ☐
25:34 ☐
26:25 ☐
26:69 ☐

Mark 1:24 ☐
5:7 ☐
6:3 ☐
14:61 ☐

Luke 23:35 ☐

John 1:29 ☐
4:42 ☐
6:35 ☐
8:12 ☐
8:24 ☐
10:7 ☐
10:11 ☐

- *the Lord* – Matthew 3:3

- *my beloved Son* – Matthew 3:17

- *the Son of God* – Matthew 4:3

- *the Lord your God* – Matthew 4:7

- *teacher* – Matthew 8:19

- *the Son of Man* – Matthew 8:20

- *the bridegroom* – Matthew 9:15

- *Lord of the Sabbath* – Matthew 12:8

- *the Son of the living God* – Matthew 16:16

- *the prophet* – Matthew 21:11

- *the King* – Matthew 25:34

- *Rabbi* – Matthew 26:25

- *Jesus the Galilean* – Matthew 26:69

- *the Holy One of God* – Mark 1:24

- *the Son of the Most High God* – Mark 5:7

- *the carpenter* – Mark 6:3

- *the son of Mary* – Mark 6:3

- *the brother of James, Joses, Judas and Simon and of his all sisters* – Mark 6:3

- *the Son of the Blessed* – Mark 14:61

- *the chosen of God* – Luke 23:35

- *the Lamb of God* – John 1:29

- *the Saviour of the world* – John 4:42

- *the bread of life* – John 6:35

- *the light of the world* – John 8:12

- *the I am* – John 8:24

- *the door of the sheep* – John 10:7

- *the good shepherd* – John 10:11

- *the resurrection and the life* – John 11:25

- *the way, the truth and the life* – John 14:6

- *the true vine* – John 15:1

- *my Lord and my God* – John 20:28

- *the Holy One and the Just* – Acts 3:14

- *the Prince of life* – Acts 3:15

- *the Prince and Saviour* – Acts 5:31

- *the Lord Jesus Christ* – Acts 28:31

- *our Passover* – 1 Corinthians 5:7

- *the head of the church* – Ephesians 5:23

- *the King of kings and Lord of lords* – 1 Timothy 6:15

- *the author of salvation* – Hebrews 2:10

- *the apostle and high priest* – Hebrews 3:1

- *the Captain of salvation* – Hebrews 12:24

- *the Lord of glory* – James 2:1

- *the Chief Shepherd* – 1 Peter 5:4

- *the Word of life* – 1 John 1:1

- *the faithful witness, the first born from the dead* – Revelation 1:5

- *the Alpha and the Omega, the First and the Last* – Revelation 1:17

- *the Amen* – Revelation 3:14

- *the Lion of the tribe of Judah, the Root of David* – Revelation 5:5

- *Faithful and True* – Revelation 19:11

- *the Bright and Morning Star* – Revelation 22:16

Even though most of these are used only once or twice in the New Testament, nearly all have specific Old Testament backgrounds. We could learn much about the Son's nature and mission through a careful study of these names and titles, but we would need to consider their scriptural backgrounds if we wanted to appreciate their insights at all correctly.

John 11:25 ☐
14:6 ☐
15:1 ☐
20:28 ☐

Acts 3:14–15 ☐
5:31 ☐
28:31 ☐

1 Corinthians 5:7 ☐

Ephesians 5:23 ☐

1 Timothy 6:15 ☐

Hebrews 2:10 ☐
3:1 ☐
12:24 ☐

James 2:1 ☐

1 Peter 5:4 ☐

1 John 1:1 ☐

Revelation 1:5 ☐
1:17 ☐
3:14 ☐
5:5 ☐
19:11 ☐
22:16 ☐

Four of the titles, however, are used with great frequency in the New Testament. Jesus is often called 'the Christ', or 'the Son of Man', or 'the Lord', or 'the Son of God', and these teach us much about his unique character and calling.

Although it may be an over-simplification to suggest that each of these titles points to either his full humanity or his full divinity, it is broadly true that 'the Christ' and 'the Son of Man' focus more on his humanity and that 'the Lord' and 'the Son of God' stress his divinity.

THE CHRIST

The Greek word *Christos* means 'the Anointed Man', and is the equivalent of the Hebrew term 'the *Messiah*'. This shows that Jesus was a man who was specially anointed, or set apart, for a specific task.

'The Christ' is Jesus' most widely used title, and the fact that the first believers were soon described as 'Christians' illustrates its importance to the way that we know the Son.

Old Testament background

The Old Testament looks forward to a 'messianic' age which promises wonderful things for God's people. We see this, for example, in Isaiah 26–29; 40–66; Ezekiel 40–48; Daniel 12 and Joel 2:28–3:21.

Surprisingly, however, 'the Messiah' is used prophetically only in Daniel 9:25–26; at other times it refers to people who are 'anointed' for particular purposes – as in 1 Samuel 24:10; Isaiah 45:1; Lamentations 4:20; Habakkuk 3:13 and Zechariah 4:14. The story of 'anointed' Cyrus suggests five messianic principles.

- *he was specially chosen by God* – Isaiah 41:25

- *he was appointed to accomplish a redemptive purpose towards God's people* – Isaiah 45:11–13

- *he was appointed to execute God's judgement* – Isaiah 47

- *he was given dominion over the nations* – Isaiah 45:1–3

- *in all his activities, the real agent was God himself* – Isaiah 45:1–7

In the Old Testament, there are three distinct groups of people who are anointed for specific offices and service:

- *priests* – Leviticus 4:3

- *kings* – 1 Kings 19:15–16

- *prophets* – 1 Kings 19:16

These three anointed offices prepared the way for 'the Anointed Man' who will be '*the* prophet, *the* priest and *the* king' who will be chosen and anointed by God to usher in the promised messianic age.

Jesus the Messiah

Modern believers often think of 'Christ' as an additional name to Jesus: for them, he is Jesus Christ in the same way that they are John White or Janet Brown. But 'Christ' is his title, not his surname: he is Christ Jesus' or 'Jesus the Christ', in the same way that someone is 'Doctor Black' or 'Jones the Butcher'.

If we want to appreciate the significance of this title, it is helpful mentally to replace the single word 'Christ' with 'the Christ' or 'the Anointed Man' whenever we come across it. We can do this in passages like Matthew 1:18; 16:16, 20; 26:63; 27:22; Mark 8:29; 14:61; Luke 2:11, 26; 9:20; 22:67; John 4:29; 7:26–31, 40–42; 9:22; 10:24; Acts 2:36; 3:20; 4:26; 5:42; 9:22; 17:3; 18:28 and 26:23.

Although Acts 10:38 and Luke 4:18 imply that Jesus was publicly anointed as the Messiah at his baptism, Jesus rarely used this title. This may have been because the Jewish people would have misunderstood this to mean that he was a political deliverer.

Jesus did accept the title when Peter recognised him as the Messiah in Mark 8:27–30, but he ordered the disciples to keep the news quiet. And he did admit that he was the Messiah when the high priest asked him, in Mark 14:61–64, whether he was the Christ.

This admission led to Jesus' death-sentence – which was swiftly reversed by God, who raised him from the dead, exalted him on high, and proclaimed the crucified Jesus as 'Lord and Messiah'. We see this in Acts 2:36 and Romans 1:4.

Jesus was a quite different 'prophet, priest and king' from the one that the Jews were expecting. They believed that the Christ would be

Leviticus 4:3 ☐

1 Kings 19:15–16 ☐

Matthew 1:18 ☐
16:16–20 ☐
26:63 ☐
27:22 ☐

Mark 8:29 ☐
14:61 ☐

Luke 2:11, 26 ☐
9:20 ☐
22:67 ☐

John 4:29 ☐
7:26–31 ☐
7:40–42 ☐
9:22 ☐
10:24 ☐

Acts 2:36 ☐
3:20 ☐
4:26 ☐
5:42 ☐
9:22 ☐
17:3 ☐
18:28 ☐
26:23 ☐

Acts 10:38 ☐

Luke 4:18 ☐

Mark 8:27–30 ☐
14:61–64 ☐

Acts 2:36 ☐

Romans 1:4 ☐

another mighty ruler like anointed David. And, in fact, the heavenly voice at Jesus' baptism, in Mark 1:11, did acclaim him as the messianic Son of Psalm 2. But, by quickly adding words from Isaiah 42:1, the voice made it plain that Jesus' anointing would be manifested as much through suffering service as through royal ruling.

The early church

The early church constantly referred to Jesus as the Christ, and this was the essential content of their preaching – especially to Jews. We see this, for example, in Acts 3:16–18; 4:10, 26; 5:42; 8:5, 12; 9:20–22; 10:36–38; 11:17; 17:3; 18:5; 24:24 and 28:31.

Acts 9:20–22 shows that Paul's recognition of Jesus as Messiah was fundamental to his conversion, and he goes on to name Jesus as Christ throughout his epistles.

As an educated Jew, Paul would have shared the common Jewish expectation that the Messiah would be a political deliverer – and Jesus' death, therefore, would have been proof that he was not the Christ.

For Paul, however, the resurrection changed everything: it proved that Jesus was God's Anointed Man, and it revealed that he had come to inaugurate a spiritual kingdom which was open to all rather than a physical kingdom which was open only to Jews.

As Peter was the first disciple to recognise Jesus as Christ, it is not surprising that he makes much of Jesus' anointing in his preaching in Acts and in his epistles. Passages like 1 Peter 1:3, 11, 19; 2:21–25; 3:18–21; 4:1, 13; 5:1 show that the early church proclaimed Jesus as the Messiah who is simultaneously both the suffering servant and the risen Lord who has conquered death. In many ways, this repeats the heavenly revelation which was given at Jesus' baptism.

Son of David

The title 'the Son of David' is closely associated with 'the Christ', because the Old Testament reveals that the Messiah will be a king who is physically descended from David.

We see this, for example, in 2 Samuel 7:16; Jeremiah 30:9; 33:15; Ezekiel 34:23–31; 37:24 and Hosea 3:5.

Matthew and Luke both trace Jesus back to David in their genealogies to establish his eligibility as Christ, and Luke 1:32, 69 prophetically reveal Jesus to be David's long-awaited descendent.

People call Jesus 'Son of David' in Matthew 9:27; 12:23; 15:22 and 21:15. These passages suggest that the miracles caused the people to hope that Jesus was powerful enough to be the coming deliverer, but they do not seem to have identified him as the Messiah.

Jesus never publicly identified himself as the Son of David, not even in Matthew 22:41–46; equally, he never rejected the title when people gave it to him.

When the early church were preaching to Jews, it was important for them to establish Jesus' credentials as Messiah by demonstrating his descent from David: we see this, for example, in Acts 13:16–23; Romans 1:3 and 2 Timothy 2:8.

This 'human lineage' proved that he was humanly qualified to fulfil God's covenant promises to David and to rule as a human king with royal authority. This is stressed in Revelation 3:7; 5:5 and 22:16.

The Servant

We have seen that the heavenly voice at Jesus' baptism introduced Jesus as both the anointed ruler of Psalm 2 who would fulfil David's covenant blessings and as the beloved suffering Servant of Isaiah 42. This means that our understanding of Jesus as 'the Christ' must embrace both the royal authority of 'the Son of David' and the sacrificial serving of 'the Servant of God'.

Although the actual title 'the Servant of God' was never used by Jesus, and is never given to him in the Gospels, it is plain that they considered him to be the special person who is referred to in Isaiah's four 'servant songs' – 42:1–4; 49:1–6; 50:4–9 and 52:13–53:12.

Isaiah prophesied that this servant would be called by God and given his Spirit; that he would restore Israel and establish justice; that he would act universally and declare his judgement among the nations; but that he would have to suffer vicariously to achieve his purpose.

Acts 3:13, 26 and 4:27–30 show that the early church regarded Jesus as this servant, and many phrases from the four servant songs are applied to Jesus – for example, in Matthew 8:17; 12:18–21; 20:28;

Luke 1:32, 69 ☐

Matthew 9:27 ☐
12:23 ☐
15:22 ☐
21:15 ☐
22:41–46 ☐

Acts 13:16–23 ☐
Romans 1:3 ☐
2 Timothy 2:8 ☐
Revelation 3:7 ☐
5:5 ☐
22:16 ☐

Isaiah 42:1–4 ☐
49:1–6 ☐
50:4–9 ☐
52:13– ☐
53:12 ☐
Acts 3:13, 26 ☐
4:27–30 ☐
Matthew 8:17 ☐
12:18–21 ☐
20:28 ☐

Mark 9:12; 10:45; Luke 22:37; Romans 4:25; 8:32–34; Hebrews 9:28; 1 Peter 1:10–11; 2:21–25 and 3:18.

The idea that Jesus is God's suffering servant is reflected in some of his other names and titles. For example, the descriptive titles *the Lamb of God*, *the Chosen One*, *the Beloved* and *the Just* are all derived from the servant songs.

THE SON OF MAN

The Gospels report that Jesus' usually described himself as 'the Son of Man'. Interestingly, they do not record anyone else describing Jesus in this way, and the title is hardly used in the rest of the New Testament.

Scholars are not sure what the title means or where it comes from. Some think it shows that Jesus was claiming to be a representative human; others insist it reveals that he considered himself *the* representative human; while many believe it merely refers to Psalm 8:4–8 and Daniel 7:13. We can grasp the title's true meaning only by recognising how Jesus used it.

Jesus seems to have used the title 'the Son of Man' in three distinct ways:

1. to refer to the work of the Son of Man on earth:

    *   *his authority* – Mark 2:10, 28; John 9:35–39

    *   *his way of living* – Matthew 8:20; 11:19

    *   *his significance* – Matthew 12:32

    *   *his ministry* – Matthew 13:37; Luke 19:10; 22:48; John 6:27

2. to refer to the sufferings of the Son of Man:

    *   *to predict his death* – Mark 8:31; 9:9, 12, 31; 10:33; Luke 11:30; John 8:28; 12:23–24

    *   *to show the significance of his death* – Mark 10:45; John 3:13–14; 6:53

    *   *to predict his betrayal* – Mark 14:21, 41

3.   to refer to the future work and glorification of the Son of Man:

- *to describe his return* – Matthew 24:37–39, 44; Mark 8:38; 13:26; 14:62; Luke 17:22–30; 18:8

- *to reveal his work* – Matthew 13:41; Luke 12:8; John 1:51; 5:27–30

- *to show his glory* – Matthew 19:28; 25:31; Luke 21:36

It is plain that this third use of the title is very closely identified with the Daniel 7:13 figure, and that the first and second use relate to Isaiah's suffering servant.

This suggests that, just as 'the Christ' encapsulates both the majesty of 'the Son of David' and the meekness of 'the Servant', so too 'the Son of Man' synthesises the glory of Daniel's prophetic person with the sacrifice of Isaiah's suffering servant: this synthesis is particularly clear in Mark 10:45.

When we take an overview of the way that Jesus uses this title, we can see that it highlights three complementary aspects of his character.

- *his unique authority* – to forgive sins, to oversee the Sabbath, to participate in the judgement, to acknowledge people before God

- *his unique humility* – he suffered at the hands of others, he had nowhere to live; he would not enjoy any material advantages of his title, and he did not expect his followers to do so either

- *his unique glory* – he spoke often about the glory associated with the Son of Man's future coming; he declared that his sufferings were a certain path to future glory; John 1:51; 3:13 and 6:62 show that this glory will not be a new experience, as it is his by right

Surprisingly, the 'Son of Man' title is used in the New Testament only four times outside the Gospels.

- *Stephen used it in Acts 7:56 at his death to emphasise the glory of the ascended Son and his exalted heavenly position.*

- *Hebrews 2:6–8 quotes Psalm 8:4–6 as part of its general establishment of Jesus' humanity as an essential characteristic of his high priestly function*

- *Revelation 1:13 and 14:14 use it in a similar way to Daniel 7:13 to describe a heavenly person who appears in a human form.*

Matthew 24:37–39 ☐
24:44 ☐

Mark 8:38 ☐
13:26 ☐
14:62 ☐

Luke 17:22–30 ☐
18:8 ☐

Matthew 13:41 ☐

Luke 12:8 ☐

John 1:51 ☐
5:27–30 ☐

Matthew 19:28 ☐
25:31 ☐

Luke 21:36 ☐

Daniel 7:13 ☐

Mark 10:45 ☐

John 1:51 ☐
3:13 ☐
6:62 ☐

Acts 7:56 ☐

Hebrews 2:6–8 ☐

Psalm 8:4–6 ☐

Revelation 1:13 ☐
14:14 ☐

The human Jesus

We have seen that the New Testament points to Jesus' full humanity by recording a host of small facts and incidental details, and by identifying him as 'the Christ' (the Anointed Man) and 'the Son of Man'.

These titles complement each other; and we can say that, in general, 'the Christ' refers essentially to *who Jesus is* as the Son (the Anointed, the Beloved, the Chosen, the long-awaited prophet, priest and king, and so on); and that 'the Son of Man' points to *what he does* as the Son (he comes from heaven, he forgives, he heals, he suffers, he dies, he judges, he returns to heaven, he will return in glory, and so on).

As we move on to consider the Son's full divinity, and to see how we can know him personally (as well as propositionally), we must not forget that he is fully human, and that he has – in principle – faced every problem and temptation that we have to face.

When we respond to his call to 'follow me', we can be certain that he does not call us to follow him anywhere that he has not been, to do anything that he has not done, to say anything that he has not said, to endure anything that he has not endured, or to face anything that he has not faced.

PART TWO

the fully divine son

We have seen that the New Testament describes Jesus as a real human being: it shows that he was born in the usual human manner; that he lived, breathed and died like all other people; that he experienced pain and pressure, hunger and tiredness, joy and grief, trials and temptation in exactly the same way that we do today.

But the Bible also insists that Jesus was more than fully human, that he was more, even, than the perfect, sinless human, for it declares that he was fully divine *and* fully human, that he was God in human flesh.

John's Gospel reveals Jesus' divinity particularly clearly, and it does this essentially by introducing him as 'the Word of God', the *logos* who is a personal self-revelation of God, and by recording a series of '*I am*' sayings in which Jesus seems to identify himself with *Yahweh*, with the ultimate 'I am who I am'.

We have seen that two of Jesus' commonest names and titles also focus on his divinity. He is presented as '*the Son of God*' throughout the New Testament; and all twenty seven books ring with the great cry that '*Jesus is Lord*'. When we take these four phrases together, we can begin to appreciate the Son's fully divine nature.

LOGOS

We consider the *logos* of God, the 'Word' of God, in some detail in *Living Faith* and *Listening to God*, and see that *logos* refers to the full self-revelation of God. These two books in *the Sword of the Spirit* series establish that God reveals himself fully through both the Scriptures (his written *logos*) and the Son (his personal *logos*).

The Greek word *logos* is one of John's Gospel's most distinctive words. Although *logos* sometimes means Jesus' message and sometimes points to Jesus himself, it always means something more than just the words spoken. John 5:24 and 8:31, 51, for example, show that God's *logos* needs to be heard and understand correctly so that its deeper 'self-revelatory' aspect is appreciated.

John's Gospel begins with the Son's 'heavenly genealogy' in 1:1–18; this makes it clear that the fully human Jesus is also the eternal Word, the full revelation of the fully divine God.

We see in *Living Faith* that the idea of God's Word is firmly rooted in the Old Testament. It reveals, for example, that God's Word:

- *is involved in creating and sustaining the world* – Genesis 1; Psalm 33:6–9; 147:15–18; 148:8

- *is invested with divine power and authority* – Psalm 147:15; Isaiah 55:11; Hosea 6:5

- *reveals God's thoughts, concerns and purposes* – Psalm 119:9, 105; Jeremiah 20:9; Ezekiel 33:7

- *is closely identified with God's Wisdom* – Job 28:12–27; Proverbs 8:1–9, 12

By identifying Jesus from the outset as the *logos*, John's Gospel implicitly declares that Jesus was involved in creation, that he is invested with divine power, that he is the revelation of God, and that he is closely identified with God's wisdom: all these ideas are then developed throughout John's Gospel.

John's 'prologue' introduces a whole series of concepts which are expanded in the Gospel (such as light, life, truth, glory and the world), but it contains three basic ideas about Jesus which reveal the main characteristics of the Son as *the logos*.

1. *his relation with the Father*

John 1:1–2 echoes Genesis 1:1 and declares the Son's pre-existence. John simply states that the *logos* was with God and was God: this underlines the Son's divinity without blurring the distinction between the personal quality of the Son and the personal quality of God.

John 1:1–2 ☐
Genesis 1:1 ☐

John 1:1–2 reveals both that the *logos* has the nature of God, and that the *logos* and God are not interchangeable terms. Although the Word is God, God is more than the Word.

2. *his relation with the world*

John 1:3, like Colossians 1:15, points to the Son's relationship with the world. This is developed throughout John's Gospel, and we consider this fully in *Reaching the Lost*. We should recognise that John does not distinguish between the creative power of the Son and the creative power of God, but that he does distinguish the Son from creation.

John 1:3 ☐
Colossians 1:15 ☐

3. *his relation with humanity*

John 1:14 explains that the divine *logos* became human flesh and dwelt among men. In *Salvation by Grace,* we see this means that God 'pitched his tent' or 'tabernacled' in humanity, and that this points directly to the Old Testament tabernacle.

John 1:14 ☐

This shows that John's proclamation of the Son as the eternal Word does not dilute Jesus' humanity; instead, it places the Son firmly in history as a flesh-and-blood human being *and* it reveals him as a divine being who is in constant and eternal communion with God.

'I AM'

John's Gospel uses the personal pronoun 'I' more frequently than any part of the Bible: this adds both dignity and authority to Jesus and to his words. John uses the Greek word *ego*, 'I', 134 times (as against 29, 17 and 23 times in Matthew, Mark and Luke) to attract attention to the Son – and to prepare us for the emphatic personal pronoun *ego eimi*, 'I am' which he seems to use to stress the Son's full divinity.

Exodus 3:14 ☐

Jesus' 'I am' sayings are important because the phrase is used in the Old Testament as God's personal name. We see in *Knowing the Father* that God introduced himself to Moses, in Exodus 3:14, as *Yahweh*, 'I am what I am'. For Jews, this invested the emphatic personal pronoun 'I am' with special divine significance.

John records seven sayings in which Jesus uses *ego eimi*, 'I am', to describe himself:

John 6:35 ☐
    8:12 ☐
    10:7 ☐
    10:11 ☐
    11:25 ☐
    14:6 ☐
    15:1 ☐

- *I am the bread of life* – 6:35

- *I am the light of the world* – 8:12

- *I am the door of the sheep* – 10:7

- *I am the good shepherd who gives his life* – 10:11

- *I am the resurrection and the life* – 11:25

- *I am the way, the truth and the life* – 14:6

- *I am the true vine* – 15:1

In every case, the 'I am' saying reveals a different divine function of Jesus – to sustain, illuminate, admit, care for sacrificially, give new life, guide and make reproductive. These are staggering claims, which are all first introduced in John's prologue. Through these seven sayings, Jesus makes personal what is declared in theory in the prologue – he reveals himself to be the divine embodiment of everything that people seek.

John 6:20 ☐
    8:24 ☐
    8:57–58 ☐
    13:19 ☐
    18:5–6 ☐

Some leaders argue that the 'I am' sayings are only an emphatic self-identification, while others suggest that they merely parallel Jesus' use of 'the Kingdom of God is like'; but John 6:20; 8:24, 58; 13:19 and 18:5 seem to refute these two suggestions.

In John 8:57–58, Jesus was asked whether he had seen Abraham. Jesus' questioners thought that his reply was blasphemous, and took up stones to kill him – they understood him to be claiming that he was the divine 'I am' of Exodus 3:14, Deuteronomy 32:39; Isaiah 43:10 and 46:4. The crowds' reaction in John 18:5–6 further underlines the divine significance of Jesus' repeated claim to be the great 'I am'.

Exodus 3:14 ☐

Deuteronomy
    32:39 ☐

Isaiah 43:10 ☐
    46:4 ☐

The force of Jesus' absolute use of *ego eimi* in John 8:24, 58 and 13:19 must shape our understanding of his seven 'I am' sayings. We can say that they convey exclusively divine qualities and functions, and that they reveal significant aspects of the Son's divine nature.

THE LORD

The Greek word *kurios*, 'lord', had many uses in the New Testament world. For example, it expressed general respect, it was a courtesy title for a superior, and it was used to address the Roman Emperor or a pagan god.

For Jews, however, *kurios* had a special meaning, as it was the Greek equivalent of their Hebrew word *Adonai* – which was one of God's root names, and was commonly used instead of *Yahweh*.

This wide usage is reflected in the New Testament: at times, 'lord' is merely a human title of respect (rather like 'Sir'), but it is more usually a divine title which emphasises the Son's divine nature as *Adonai*.

The resurrected Lord

Throughout the ages, most church leaders have believed that Jesus was recognised as *ho kurios*, 'the Lord', only after (and because of) his resurrection. This is most plain in Mark's Gospel, where the only person to address Jesus as *kurios* before the resurrection is a Syro-Phoenician woman who uses the word, in Mark 7:28, because she is a Gentile woman speaking to a strange Jewish man.

Elsewhere in Mark, wherever the other Gospels use *kurios*, Mark does not – for example, Matthew 8:2 and Mark 1:40; Matthew 8:25 and Mark 4:39; Matthew 26:22 and Mark 14:19. In contrast to this silence, Mark 16:19–20 suddenly reveals that the risen Son is now 'the Lord'.

This link of 'the Lord' with the resurrection is repeated in Luke 24:34, which seems to be Luke's explanation for his frequent use of the word throughout the Gospel – in, for example, 7:13, 19; 10:1, 39, 41; 11:39; 12:42; 13:15; 17:5–6; 18:6; 19:8; 22:61 and 24:34.

Luke's birth narrative prepares the way for Jesus' divine 'lordship' by continually describing God as Lord – in 1:9, 11, 15, 25, 32, 38, 45, 46, 58, 66, 68, 76; 2:9, 2, 23, 24, 29 and 39. We can say that, if Lord means God at the start of Luke, it surely means God throughout Luke when he uses it to describe the Son.

Because of this, we can say that the angel's identification of the Saviour in Luke 2:11 communicates divine lordship. This suggests

Mark 7:28 ☐

Matthew 8:2 ☐

Mark 1:40 ☐

Matthew 8:25 ☐

Mark 4:39 ☐

Matthew 26:22 ☐

Mark 14:19 ☐

16:19–20 ☐

Luke 7:13–19 ☐

10:1 ☐

10:39–41 ☐

11:39 ☐

12:42 ☐

13:15 ☐

17:5–6 ☐

18:6 ☐

19:8 ☐

22:61 ☐

24:34 ☐

Luke 1:9–2:39 ☐

that 'Christ the Lord' is the scriptural phrase which most neatly encapsulates both the Son's full humanity and his full divinity.

John's Gospel follows the basic pattern of identifying Jesus as 'the Lord' mainly after his resurrection. *Ho kurios* is used only three times in the first nineteen chapters, but suddenly becomes the common name for the Son in chapters twenty and twenty-one. Most strikingly, it is clearly linked with God in Thomas' John 20:28 confession of belief which seems to be the dramatic and literary climax of the Gospel.

Throughout Acts, the disciples both address the risen Son as 'Lord' (as in Acts 1:6, 24; 4:29; 9:5; 10:4, 14; 22:8, 19) and refer to him as 'Lord Jesus' or 'Lord Jesus Christ' – as in 1:21; 4:33; 7:59; 8:16; 11:17, 20; 15:11, 26; 20:21, 24, 35 and 28:31. These passages show that the first Christians were convinced that the resurrection was the proof of Jesus' divinity.

The first sermon of the Age of the Church reached its climax in Acts 2:36 with Peter's declaration that 'God has made this Jesus, whom you crucified, both Lord and Christ'. Peter's words in 2:20–21 and 34–35 show that this declaration of Jesus' divine lordship was based firmly on the Old Testament background of 'Lord' as meaning divine.

Peter's link in the first evangelistic sermon between Jesus' *divine lordship* and his *human messiahship* is crucial to our knowledge, to our experience and to our proclamation of the Son. In fact, we can say that knowing Jesus as 'the Lord and the Christ' is the main key to knowing the Son in the fullness of his unique dual nature.

Other passages in Acts, like 9:4–17 and 10:36, make it plain that Jesus' lordship means absolute authority and total sovereignty – he is either 'Lord of all' or 'not Lord at all'.

The early church

All Paul's letters proclaim that 'Jesus is Lord', and passages like Romans 10:9 show that this points essentially to his resurrection. The Son is 'Lord of all' because he has conquered death and has been raised by God to this supremely exalted position.

Quite simply, resurrection and lordship are utterly inseparable, for it is resurrection faith which provides the basis for our confession of Christ's lordship.

Paul proclaims Jesus as Lord in, for example, Romans 10:12; 1 Corinthians 12:3 and Philippians 2:11. These passages draw together the present acknowledgement of Jesus' lordship among Christians and the prospect of universal acknowledgement in the future.

In 2 Corinthians 4:5, Paul reveals that the Son's lordship is the essence of his evangelistic preaching. This suggests that any contemporary preaching which does not announce Jesus' absolute authority and total sovereignty is out of step with the scriptural revelation about the Son.

Nearly all the New Testament books stress that Jesus is Lord – for example, Romans 4:24; 1 Corinthians 6:14; 2 Corinthians 1:14; Galatians 6:14; Ephesians 6:23–24; Philippians 2:11; Colossians 2:6; 1 Thessalonians 5:9; 2 Thessalonians 1:8; 1 Timothy 1:1–2; 2 Timothy 1:2; Titus 1:4; Philemon 1:3; Hebrews 13:20; James 1:1; 1 Peter 1:3; 2 Peter 3:18; 2 John 1:3; Jude 1:17 and Revelation 11:8.

When we take an overview of the way that the New Testament presents Jesus' lordship, we can say that it uses this particular title:

- *to stress the Son's resurrection and to symbolise his conquest over death*

- *to imply that the Son is fully divine and that he fulfils the same functions as God*

- *to underline the Son's absolute authority and total sovereignty over every aspect of life and faith*

THE SON OF GOD

The fourth main New Testament title of Jesus points to his full divinity with the utmost clarity: he is 'the Son of God'. This suggests that, if we are to know the Son at all accurately, we must know him in his unique relationship with the Father.

As with every biblical revelation, we should try to understand the idea of 'the Son of God' in its scriptural context. The Old Testament prepares the way for this title by using the idea of divine sonship in several different ways, for example:

Romans 10:12 ☐

1 Corinthians 12:3 ☐

Philippians 2:11 ☐

2 Corinthians 4:5 ☐

Romans 4:24 ☐

1 Corinthians 6:14 ☐

2 Corinthians 1:14 ☐

Galatians 6:14 ☐

Ephesians 6:23–24 ☐

Philippians 2:11 ☐

Colossians 2:6 ☐

1 Thessalonians 5:9 ☐

2 Thessalonians 1:8 ☐

1 Timothy 1:1–2 ☐

2 Timothy 1:2 ☐

Titus 1:4 ☐

Philemon 1:3 ☐

Hebrews 13:20 ☐

James 1:1 ☐

1 Peter 1:3 ☐

2 Peter 3:18 ☐

2 John 1:3 ☐

Jude 1:17 ☐

Revelation 11:8 ☐

- *angels are described as sons of God, and this denotes their spiritual nature* – Genesis 6:1–4; Job 1:6; 2:1

- *Adam is identified as the son of God, again signifying his spiritual nature* – Luke 3:38

- *the Israelites were collectively called sons of God to distinguish them from surrounding nations* – Deuteronomy 14:1–2; Jeremiah 3:19–20; Hosea 1:10

- *Israel as a whole was called 'my son' to reveal the nation's unique father-son relationship with God* – Hosea 11:1

- *Israel's anointed king was in some special way God's particular son* – 2 Samuel 7:14; Psalm 2:7

We consider the Father's relationship with the Son in *Knowing the Father* and see that the Gospels record Jesus describing God as 'the Father', 'my Father', 'my heavenly Father', 'your heavenly Father' and 'Abba Father' over fifty times.

In *Knowing the Father*, we establish that Jesus had a unique relationship with the Father, and that there is an important distinction between God as 'Father of Jesus' and God as 'Father of disciples' – this is seen most clearly in John 20:28, but it can also be seen in the passages which stress that Jesus is God's 'only' Son.

We consider the Son's relationship with the Father in detail in Part Seven, but we should note now how passages like Matthew 11:25–30; Mark 1:11; 9:2–7; 12:1–12, 35–37; 13:32; Luke 10:21–24 and 22:29 reveal some of the basic elements of Jesus' divine sonship.

John's writings

As John 20:31 states that the specific purpose of the Gospel is to help readers believe that Jesus is the Son of God, we should not be surprised that this Gospel emphasises this title and the divine aspects of Jesus' nature.

Although the title 'Son of God' occurs only ten times in John's Gospel, Jesus speaks of God as 'Father' over a hundred times. Jesus' awareness of his divine sonship dominates John's Gospel, and every chapter offers at least one glimpse of what it means to be the unique Son of God.

There are four occasions in John, 1:14–18 and 3:16–18, when Jesus is described as the 'only' Son; and this proves that Jesus' sonship was not the same as ours. John 1:12 shows that we may be given power to become sons of God, but Jesus does not need this because he is a Son of a quite different kind.

Matthew 4:3–6; Luke 4:3–9, 41 record the fact that Satan and demons acknowledged Jesus as Son of God; but John gives three instances when people recognised Jesus' divine sonship – 1:34, 49 and 11:27 – and three examples of Jesus' claim to be the Son of God – 10:36–37; 11:4 and 19:7.

Although we will consider John's teaching about Jesus' divine sonship in more detail in Part Seven, we should note that this Gospel suggests several important characteristics of Jesus as Son of God:

- *the Son is sent by-and-from the Father* – 3:34; 5:36–38; 7:29; 11:42; 17:4–5

- *the Son is loved by the Father* – 3:35; 5:20; 10:17; 17:23–24

- *the Son submits to and depends on the Father* – 5:19, 30; 14:28–31; 15:10

- *the Son is absolutely one with the Father* – 5:19–23; 10:30; 14:11, 20; 17:11

- *the Son prays to the Father* – 11:41; 12:28; 17:1, 5, 11, 21, 24, 25

- *the Son is the exclusive revelation of the Father* – 6:46; 8:19; 10:15; 14:8–9

- *the Son speaks the words of the Father* – 10:18; 12:49–50; 14:24; 15:15; 16:25

- *the Son has received all things from the Father* – 8:16; 13:3; 16:15; 18:11

- *the Son will return to the Father* – 14:12, 28; 16:10, 16, 28; 20:17

The theme of Jesus as 'Son of God' also dominates 1 John, and is one of the main reasons why we can be sure that the Epistle was written by the same person as the Gospel.

1 John shows that belief in Jesus as Son of God should be a believer's chief confession – we see this, for example, in 2:22–23; 3:23;

John 1:14–18 ☐
3:16–18 ☐
John 1:12 ☐
Matthew 4:3–6 ☐
Luke 4:3–9, 41 ☐
John 1:34 ☐
1:49 ☐
11:27 ☐
10:36–37 ☐
11:4 ☐
19:7 ☐
3:34–35 ☐
5:36–38 ☐
7:29 ☐
11:42 ☐
17:4–5 ☐
5:19–23 ☐
10:15–18 ☐
17:23–24 ☐
5:30 ☐
14:28–31 ☐
15:10 ☐
10:30 ☐
14:8–12 ☐
14:20 ☐
17:11 ☐
11:41 ☐
12:28 ☐
17:1–25 ☐
6:46 ☐
8:16–19 ☐
12:49–50 ☐
14:24–28 ☐
15:15 ☐
16:25 ☐
13:3 ☐
16:10–16 ☐
18:11 ☐
16:28 ☐
20:17 ☐
1 John 2:22–23 ☐
3:23 ☐
4:15 ☐
5:5 ☐

4:15; 5:5 and 5:10–13. Other aspects of Jesus' sonship are stressed in 1 John 1:7; 3:8; 4:9–10, 14; 5:9–11 and 20.

Paul's teaching

Acts 9:20 reports that the apostle Paul's first sermons proclaimed the vital truth that Jesus was both 'the Christ' and 'the Son of God' – that he was both human and divine. And Romans 1:1–4 introduces the concept of Jesus as 'Son of God' which is the basic assumption behind Paul's presentation of Jesus.

Some leaders have suggested Romans 1:4 means that Jesus was not the Son of God before the resurrection; but this is not true. Instead, Romans 1:4 shows that the resurrection revealed publicly what was already an established fact.

We can say that the disciples had a much better appreciation of Jesus as Son of God after the resurrection, but this is quite different from suggesting that Jesus became the Son of God through the resurrection.

It should be clear that Jesus' sonship is an essential, eternal relationship within the triune God which, therefore, was not fundamentally altered either by the incarnation or by the ascension. We consider the relationships within the Godhead in some detail in *Knowing the Father*.

Paul identifies Jesus as 'Son of God' only in 2 Corinthians 1:19; Galatians 2:20 and Ephesians 4:13; he more usually describes Jesus as 'his Son' – for example, Romans 1:9; 8:29; 1 Corinthians 1:9; Ephesians 4:13; Galatians 4:6 and Colossians 1:13.

For Paul, Jesus' divine sonship is totally linked with Jesus' mission: so, for example, in Romans 8:3 and Galatians 4:4–5 he describes how God sent his Son into the sinful world to redeem humanity. We consider this fully in Part Five.

Paul also stresses the practical effects of Jesus' sonship on believers. In Romans 8:15 and Galatians 3:26–4:7, for example, he describes our position as sons of God and shows how this has come about.

These passages provide a valuable insight into the intimate relationship between the Father and the Son; they also suggest that this relationship is a pattern for God's relationship with us.

JESUS IS GOD

We have seen that the New Testament reveals Jesus' divinity by introducing him as 'the Word of God', by recording a series of 'I am' sayings in which Jesus seems to identify himself with *Yahweh*, and by presenting him as 'Lord of all' and 'Son of God'.

There are, however, a few important passages which go even further and declare that Jesus is God in the plainest of language. For example:

- John's Gospel opens and closes with clear statements of Jesus' divine nature. John 1:1 affirms that the *logos* not only was with God but also was God – this is amplified in 1:18. And John 20:28 is the Gospel's wonderful climax of belief – truly Jesus is both 'Lord' and 'God'.

  John 1:1 ☐
  1:18 ☐
  20:28 ☐

- Romans 9:5 is Paul's strongest statement about Jesus' divinity, yet it is weakened by some English versions of the Bible which punctuate it inaccurately. There are several compelling grammatical reasons for insisting that the translators of the New King James Version and the New Jerusalem Bible are correct, and that the translators of the New International Version and the Revised Standard Version are mistaken.

  Romans 9:5 ☐

- Titus 2:13 is similarly absolute. Paul plainly refers to 'our great God and Saviour Jesus Christ' and not to (as some suggest) 'our great God and our Saviour Jesus Christ'. If Paul had meant to differentiate 'God' and 'Jesus' he would have added a second article, and he would not have used the same expression ('God our Saviour') in Titus 1:3.

  Titus 2:13 ☐

  Titus 1:3 ☐

- Hebrews 1:8 quotes Psalm 45:6 and applies it in such a way to show that the Son is being addressed as God. Whatever the original meaning of the Psalm, the writer of Hebrews was inspired to use it to identify the Son as God.

  Hebrews 1:8 ☐
  Psalm 45:6 ☐

- 2 Peter 1:1 is another simple declaration that Jesus Christ is both God and Saviour.

  2 Peter 1:1 ☐

These verses demonstrate that the early church knew the fully human Jesus was also fully divine. We see this belief in action in those passages which record that worship normally given to God is sometimes given to Christ – for example, Matthew 28:9; 2 Timothy 4:18;

Matthew 28:9 ☐

2 Timothy 4:18 ☐

2 Peter 3:18 ☐

Revelation 1:5–6 ☐

5:13 ☐

7:10 ☐

Acts 7:59–60 ☐

1 Corinthians
16:22 ☐

2 Corinthians
12:8 ☐

1 Thessalonians
3:11–12 ☐

2 Thessalonians
3:5, 16 ☐

2 Peter 3:18; Revelation 1:5–6; 5:13 and 7:10; in those passages which describe prayers being addressed to Jesus – for example, Acts 7:59–60; 1 Corinthians 16:22 and 2 Corinthians 12:8; and in those benedictions which link his name with the name of God – for example, 1 Thessalonians 3:11–12 and 2 Thessalonians 3:5, 16.

Fully human, fully divine

In the first two parts of this book, we have seen that the New Testament presents a straightforward paradox. It declares that Jesus of Nazareth was a genuine human being who claimed to be, and was, *Adonai Yahweh*, the Lord God; it reveals that he was simultaneously both a transcendent, pre-existent divine being who came to save humanity and a perfect, sinless human being who showed humanity how to live.

The New Testament, however, does not go on to explain how Jesus could be God and be distinguishable from God, or how he could become human without modifying his divinity to such an extent that he ceased to be truly divine, or how the two aspects of his nature came to co-exist within him. It simply declares the dual nature of Jesus and leaves the rest to faith.

People have struggled with this paradox throughout church history. Some have sought to concentrate on knowing the fully divine Son; others have found it easier to focus on the fully human Son; while still more have tried to simplify the paradox through unbiblical ideas like 'adoptionism', 'kenoticism' and 'docetism'.

When, however, we take any of these approaches the inevitable result is that we do not know the Son who is revealed in the Scriptures.

No matter how hard it is to comprehend the biblical doctrine of Christ with our minds, we must not move away from the essential New Testament paradox. Instead, we can be sure that, as we grapple with God's Word with our minds, and as we open our spirits to God's written *logos*, so the Spirit of God's Son will enable us to know the Son in the full wonder of his unique dual nature.

PART THREE

a unique being

Everybody knows that the New Testament contains four accounts of the life and death of Jesus Christ. The books of Matthew, Mark, Luke and John are the perfect work of God the Spirit in portraying the nature and mission of God the Son: each verse of every Gospel is God-breathed and vital for guiding our lives and teaching us his way to live.

The four Gospels communicate the truth about the Son's unique being in the fullest possible way by describing his life and mission from slightly different, but complementary, perspectives.

The first four books of the New Testament do not merely corroborate each other (though they do), for they are more than repetitive testimonies. Each has its own objective, and makes its own selection and arrangement of facts; each has distinctive themes, and stresses different aspects of the message of Jesus; and each includes material which is unique to that Gospel, and appears to ignore some incidents and details that the writer must have known about.

This all came about under the careful guidance and inspiration of the Spirit, and it means that we need to appreciate all four Gospels to know God's *Personal Word* in the way that his *Written Word* reveals.

MATTHEW

Throughout his Gospel, Matthew presents Jesus essentially as a king who has come to found a kingdom: he highlights issues of leadership and authority, and focuses on God's heavenly kingdom.

Matthew establishes Jesus' royal credentials by placing a genealogy at the start of the Gospel; he traces Jesus' descent from Abraham, through David and the line of Israel's kings, to Joseph, Jesus' *official* father.

Matthew 1:18–2:23 ☐

In his 1:18–2:23 account of the nativity, Matthew underlines the theme of authority, illustrates Jesus' kingship, and sheds light on the mystery of God's developing kingdom. The action centres on Joseph (the head of the household) and stresses his perfect obedience; Bethlehem is identified as the promised location from which a leader will come to rule God's people; great men of the east seek a new king; and the news of a royal birth alarms the Jewish king Herod.

Matthew seems to portray the nativity as a conflict between kings and different ways of ruling: the powerful usurper attempts to deceive the Wise Men, tries to kill Jesus, and murders the children of Bethlehem; whereas the rightful heir is peaceful, vulnerable, gentle – and is protected by God who works through obedient humans.

Matthew 5–7 ☐
10 ☐
13 ☐
18 ☐
24–25 ☐
8:1–9:37 ☐
16:18–19 ☐
18:15–20 ☐
21:1–16 ☐
22:1–14 ☐
23:1–39 ☐

Matthew records five blocks of authoritative teaching by Jesus (5–7; 10; 13; 18; 24–25), and this appears to parallel the five books of the Jewish Law. These teaching passages focus on the themes of 'the kingdom of heaven' and 'righteousness' to reveal the heavenly character and moral authority of the royal Son.

Matthew also gathers together ten miracles in 8:1–9:37 to illustrate the physical and spiritual authority of God's kingdom. These reveal Jesus as ruler over nature, ruler over disease and ruler over demons.

Matthew is the only Gospel to mention 'the church', and 16:18–19 and 18:15–20 teach that the church will be given royal power and heavenly authority.

In 21:1–16, Matthew reports Jesus' entry into Jerusalem as a king more fully than the other Gospels. He follows this, in 22:1–14, with a parable which shows that the king can choose whom he likes to enter his kingdom; with a unique indictment, in 23:1–39, of the scribes and

Pharisees who abuse their authority and live unrighteously; and, in 24:1–25:46, with some detailed teaching about the second coming of the king who will return with universal authority to judge and rule.

In his record of Jesus' passion and resurrection, in 26:1–28:20, Matthew gives a full account of Jesus' trial by the Roman Governor, and makes much of Pilate's question in 27:11 and the soldiers' mocking cries in 27:29. He then reports several distinctive details which underline the unique power and authority of Jesus' death and resurrection – he alone describes, for example:

- *the supernatural earthquake – 27:51*

- *the opening of the tombs – 27:52*

- *the resurrected holy people – 27:52*

- *the guards – 27:62–65*

- *the seals on the stone – 27:66*

- *the violent earthquake – 28:2*

- *the angel who rolls the stone away – 28:2*

- *the women who bow down before Jesus – 28:9*

- *the women who obey Jesus – 28:10–11*

- *the unrighteous authorities who lie – 28:11–15*

Finally, Matthew closes his Gospel by selecting words, in 28:18 and 28:20, which re-emphasise the Son's royal authority and call again for whole-hearted obedience in the lives of Jesus' subjects.

MARK

Mark's Gospel does not so much present the Son as a powerful king who comes to reign, but more as a suffering servant who comes to serve and offer himself as a sacrifice for all humanity. Throughout his short account of the Son's unique mission, Mark delicately highlights many small details of Jesus' life which, when taken together, seem to suggest the perfect example of patient service.

Matthew 24:1–
    25:46 ☐
    26:1–
    28:20 ☐

Mark does not record a family tree or any details about Jesus' birth – for him, it is not the origin of servants which matters but the work that they do and how well they do it. In contrast to the other Gospels, Mark passes quickly over Jesus' baptism, offers no details about his testing in the desert, and goes straight to his service in Galilee.

Mark does not report any occasion when Jesus makes an extended kingly proclamation of the laws of his kingdom, and he describes very few of the Son's judgements – for Mark, service lies more in doing than in speaking. He mentions only eight short parables, and most of these have an obvious connection with service.

Mark seems to use the Greek word *euthus*, 'at once' or 'immediately', to underline his theme of service. *Euthus* appears eighty times in the New Testament, and over half of these occur in Mark – where it appears to suggest the quick response of an eager servant.

Mark mentions many small details about Jesus' life which are omitted by the other Gospels in their accounts of the same incidents. These are the sort of details which are noticed only by those with the eyes of a servant who notes and admires discreet service in others – for example:

- *he took her by the hand and lifted her up* – 1:31
- *he looked around at them with anger* – 3:5
- *they went into a house* – 3:19
- *he looked around in a circle at those who sat about him* – 3:34
- *he had entered a house* – 7:17
- *he turned around and looked at his disciples* – 8:33
- *he took him by the hand and lifted him up* – 9:27
- *he had come into the house* – 9:28
- *he took him in his arms* – 9:36
- *he took them up in his arms* – 10:16
- *he was going out on the road* – 10:17
- *Jesus, looking at him, loved him* – 10:21
- *he followed Jesus on the road* – 10:52
- *he was walking in the temple* – 11:27

Mark 1:31 ☐
3:5 ☐
3:19 ☐
3:34 ☐
7:17 ☐
8:33 ☐
9:27–28 ☐
9:36 ☐
10:16–17 ☐
10:21 ☐
10:52 ☐
11:27 ☐

In 7:31–37 and 8:22–26, Mark describes two miracles which are not mentioned elsewhere, and uses them to reveal Jesus' desire to work unobtrusively. In Mark, the Son wants to serve unseen, is ready to serve unthanked, asks for secrecy, and tries to hide himself – as in 7:24.

A good servant, however, is usually at the beck-and-call of others, and Mark shows how the Son allows people to intrude on his privacy in 1:35–39; 3:20; 6:31–34, 45 and 54–55.

Mark does not ignore Jesus' power and authority, but he refers to it more briefly than Matthew – and he offers some exclusive insights, in 1:35, 41; 6:34 and 10:21, which suggest key secrets of Jesus' power.

Mark goes into more detail than the other Gospels about the difficulties which were felt and faced by the Son – for example, 3:5, 21; 6:6; 7:34 and 8:12. Jesus' greatest suffering took place on the cross, and a deep awareness of the cross pervades this Gospel.

Throughout Mark, the cross is revealed as both the price and the glory of service. Everything leads towards the moment in chapter eight when the apostles finally realise who Jesus is and are ready to learn about the cross. From this point on, the theme of suffering and death dominates the Gospel – we see this, for example, in 10:21, 30 and 45.

Mark concludes his Gospel quite differently to the other writers by showing that the risen Son is still a servant. We have already seen that, in 16:20, Mark suddenly identifies Jesus as 'the Lord'; we should, however, also note Mark's quiet reminder that the risen Lord is still serving with the disciples on earth, and is still confirming the Word through accompanying signs. With this characteristic small touch, Mark closes his account of the serving Son.

LUKE

Luke's Gospel does not present the Son primarily as either a king or a servant, but more as the ideal human being – as the perfect specimen of humanity, as the pattern life for all humankind.

Luke stresses that Jesus is someone who is tested in every possible way, who is subject to ordinary conflict and emotions, and yet who

Mark 7:31–37 ☐
8:22–26 ☐
7:24 ☐
1:35–39 ☐
3:20 ☐
6:31–34 ☐
6:45 ☐
6:54–55 ☐
1:41 ☐
6:34 ☐
10:21 ☐
3:5 ☐
3:21 ☐
6:6 ☐
7:34 ☐
8:12 ☐
10:21 ☐
10:30 ☐
10:45 ☐
16:20 ☐

Luke 1:5–2:38 ☐
3:23–38 ☐

Luke 3:1–2, 19 ☐
4:16 ☐
1:31–33 ☐
3:15–17 ☐
3:22 ☐
4:17–23 ☐
7:18–20 ☐
8:25 ☐
9:7–9 ☐
9:20–21 ☐

Luke 3:10–11 ☐
7:5–6 ☐
8:1–3 ☐
19:8–10 ☐
21:1–4 ☐
23:50–54 ☐

Luke 5:1–11 ☐
12:33–34 ☐

Luke 2:16–24 ☐
9:58 ☐
23:53 ☐

Luke 3:21 ☐
5:16 ☐
6:12 ☐
9:18, 28 ☐
11:1–8 ☐
18:1–14 ☐
19:45–46 ☐
22:32–45 ☐
23:46 ☐
24:30–31 ☐

remains without sin. We can say that this Gospel reveals the Son to be *the* sympathetic friend of sinners and *the* person to be followed.

Luke makes much of the events surrounding Jesus' birth, and uses the story to introduce some of his distinctive themes: Jesus' humanity, the place of women, the treatment of the poor, care for small children, the help of the Holy Spirit, hospitality, healing miracles, praise and joy.

In 1:5–2:38, Luke shows that God wants to draw ordinary people to himself, to fill them with the Spirit, and to use them in passing on good news about Jesus. In 3:23–38, Luke traces Jesus' ancestors back to Adam to show that Jesus is the brother of all humanity.

Luke's account of the nativity focuses on Mary's response to God; on shepherds who visit empty-handed; on his parents' poverty; on the miracles which affect lowly Zacharias; and on the Holy Spirit, praise and joy – for example, 1:14, 28, 44, 47, 58, 64; 2:10, 13, 20 and 38.

Luke alone sets the Son's historical and political background – 3:1–2, 19; 4:16. In the first part of his Gospel, he offers several clues to Jesus' identity and presents many people who wonder who Jesus can be – for example, 1:31–33; 3:15–17, 22; 4:17–22, 23; 7:18–20; 8:25 and 9:7–9. All this leads to 9:20–21, when Luke unveils Jesus as 'the Christ of God'.

Luke focuses on the Son's teaching about money, and often makes a financial observation about the people he describes – as in 3:10–11; 7:5–6; 8:1–3; 19:8–10; 21:1–4 and 23:50–54. Most of Luke's unique parables are about wealth, and even the unique miracle he reports in 5:1–11 is, in part, an economic test: will they leave the bumper catch on the shore for others while they themselves follow Jesus? This emphasis is best expressed in 12:33–34: if righteousness is the most important kingdom characteristic for Matthew, generosity is its equivalent for Luke.

For Luke, the Son is someone who is clearly on the side of the lowest members of society: his first resting place is an animal feeding trough, his last is another man's grave, and in between he has nowhere to lay his head: Luke even reports that Jesus' parents had to make the special offering for the poor – we see this in 2:16, 24; 9:58 and 23:53.

It is Luke who reveals that the Son is a person of prayer: John may record Jesus' longest prayer, and Matthew may go into more detail about the Lord's Prayer, but Luke shows that prayer fills every aspect of Jesus' life – we see this, for example, in 3:21; 5:16; 6:12; 9:18, 28; 11:1–8; 18:1–14; 19:45–46; 22:32, 40, 45; 23:46 and 24:30–31.

Luke's Gospel makes it clear that the Son is good news for ordinary men and women. He describes five occasions when Jesus is a guest at a meal, and some of Jesus' most challenging teaching is given in these informal settings – for example, 5:32; 7:36–50; 1:37–54; 14:1–14.

Throughout his Gospel, Luke introduces a series of people who respond to the Son in contrasting ways: he begins with a detailed description of God's dealings with Zacharias, and ends by recounting Jesus' conversation with Cleopas. Together with Zacchaeus, these are Luke's great examples of ordinary men who are transformed by God.

Luke underlines Jesus' radical attitude to women in a series of passages which reveal their place in his ministry: 7:11–16, 36–38; 8:1–3; 10:38–42; 11:27–28; 13:10–17; 15:8–10; 18:1–8; 23:49, 55 and 24:10.

Luke records about the same number of miracles as Matthew and Mark, but his selection is quite different. While they describe more powerful encounters with demons and nature, Luke concentrates on miracles of healing. He records ten unique miracles – 1:20–22, 24, 64; 5:4–7; 7:11–17; 10:17; 13:10–17; 14:1–6; 17:11–19 and 22:51.

All Luke's miracles focus on Jesus, but they are not all worked by the Son. Luke 1:20–22, 24, 64 show that God works miracles sovereignly, and Luke 9:10; 9:49–50 and 10:17 show that he can work miracles through anyone he chooses, not just through Jesus.

Luke's version of Jesus' passion is similar to the other Gospels, but with a few extra details – for example, 22:51; 22:64 and 23:39–43. Although Luke's is the briefest account, it conveys a remarkable intensity of anguish. Luke 22:42–44 describes Jesus enduring unparalleled spiritual agony as he wrestles with his Father's will: it is Luke's most telling insight into the Son's humanity.

Luke leaves it to the other Gospel writers to show that Jesus' death is 'a ransom for many' and a victory over Satan. He concentrates on revealing that Jesus' death is the ultimate example of perfect human goodness. For Luke, the cross is where the Messiah fulfils his Isaiah 53 destiny by accepting and enduring rejection, suffering and death.

This Gospel closes exactly as it opens, with an angel, a miracle and disbelief by those who should know better. Luke underlines the physical reality of Jesus' risen body, and includes an appearance to an ordinary disciple. The book then ends where it began – in the Temple – and Luke signs off with yet more words of joy.

Luke 5:32 ☐
7:36–50 ☐
1:37–54 ☐
14:1–14 ☐

Luke 7:11–16 ☐
8:1–3 ☐
10:38–42 ☐
11:27–28 ☐
13:10–17 ☐
15:8–10 ☐
18:1–8 ☐
23:49–55 ☐
24:10 ☐

Luke 1:20–22 ☐
1:24 ☐
1:64 ☐
5:4–7 ☐
7:11–17 ☐
10:17 ☐
13:10–17 ☐
14:1–6 ☐
17:11–19 ☐
22:51 ☐

Luke 9:10 ☐
9:49–50 ☐
10:17 ☐
22:51 ☐
22:64 ☐
23:39–43 ☐
22:42–44 ☐

JOHN

John is the most distinctive Gospel, for it presents Jesus not so much as the royal son of David, or the suffering servant of God, or the perfect example of humanity, but more as the glorious Son of God.

John 1:1–18 ☐

Although John knew Mary much better than the other Gospel writers, he ignores Jesus' human origins and begins his Gospel, in 1:1–18, with a heavenly genealogy. He uses words of astonishing beauty to describe the Son's relationship with God, and to make it plain that Jesus is fully divine. In this 'prologue', John introduces the distinctive themes of light, life, glory and truth which run through his Gospel.

John 1:19–2:12 ☐

In 1:19–2:12, John describes the first week of Jesus' ministry. All four Gospels describe John the Baptist's earthly relationship with Jesus, but John's Gospel shows a different side: if Jesus is 'the light', John is 'a lamp'; and if Jesus is 'the Word', the Baptist is 'a voice'.

While Matthew highlights John the Baptist's preaching about the kingdom, and Luke stresses his demands for repentance evidenced by generosity; John records his unique announcements about divine Jesus – 1:34–35. And when Matthew shows that John is reluctant to baptise Jesus because he recognises his superior authority, and Luke points out that John and Jesus are humanly related and must surely know each other; John states, in 1:33, that the Baptist does not know Jesus.

At first sight, this seems to be an insurmountable discrepancy; but we must realise that John is writing about Jesus the divine Son and not about Jesus the man. It is possible to know the Son as a human and as a servant, even as a king, and not to know him as God. John the Baptist knew Jesus as a cousin from infancy, but he did not know him as the Lamb of God until he saw the Spirit rest on him.

John's first week ends with Jesus' first sign, and he uses this miracle to hint at two ideas which he develops later in the Gospel: first, that human work always ends in failure, but that the Son brings glory out of failure; and second, that, when human provision is exhausted, the Son provides an abundant supply of good things.

John 2:13–4:54 ☐

In 2:13–4:54, John unveils a progression of spiritual ideas. First, he underlines the fact that the Son can restore whatever humanity ruins; next, he explains the miracle of new birth; and then he introduces the indwelling Spirit – we see these in 2:20; 3:3 and 4:14.

John makes it plain that the Son has come to bring life. If Matthew is concerned with righteousness and Luke with generosity, John is preoccupied with life. And if Matthew's disciples become righteous by obeying the king and Luke's become generous by imitating the man, John's disciples receive eternal life by believing in the Son.

John first mentions life and belief in 1:4 and 12; he establishes the link between them in 3:15–16; and then he weaves the two themes tightly together throughout the rest of his Gospel – for example 5:39; 6:40; 11:25–26 and 20:27–31.

John 1:4, 12 ☐
3:15–16 ☐
5:39 ☐
6:40 ☐
11:25–26 ☐
20:27–31 ☐
5:1–47 ☐

In 5:1–47, John describes a unique healing miracle to contrast the weakness of the Law with the Son's life-giving power: just as only the strongest benefit from the pool, so only the strong are helped by the Law; and just as the weakest are given strength by the Son, so anyone who believes in him receives life.

In 5:19, John offers the first glimmer into another of his distinctive themes – the oneness of the Son and the Father. From here to the end of his Gospel, he makes it clear that Jesus and the Father are one: the Son speaks what the Father says, goes where the Father sends, and does what the Father is doing. By this repetition, John stresses both the Son's submission to the Father and his union with the Father.

In 6:1–71, John describes a second Passover and presents the Son as the fulfilment of the Passover – for example, 6:35 and 54. Then, in 7:1–10:21, he describes a feast of Tabernacles and, in 7:37 and 8:12, shows Jesus to be the fulfilment of this feast too.

John 6:1–71 ☐
7:1–10:21 ☐

Until this point, John has shown the Son mainly as life, but now he starts to develop the theme of light. John uses two incidents to reveal the extraordinary nature of the Son's light. First, an adulteress stands in the light before Jesus and is not condemned, while Pharisees walk away convicted by their own consciences; then, a blind man sees. Of course, blind people are healed in the other Gospels too, but only John introduces such a miracle with Jesus' extraordinary claim in 9:5.

In 10:22–11:57, John relates Jesus to the Feast of Dedication – which celebrated the great Jewish victory under the Maccabees in the period between the Old and New Testaments. This was the perfect setting for the Son's announcement of his great victory over death which he signified with Lazarus' raising from the dead. In this passage, John re-emphasises all his distinctive themes – 10:30, 38; 11:10, 25–26 and 40.

John 10:22–11:57 ☐

John 13:1, 34 ☐

14:21 ☐

15:13 ☐

16:27 ☐

17:26 ☐

John 14:27 ☐

18:4–6 ☐

20:27–31 ☐

Most of this Gospel is quite different from the other three Gospels, but John's long report of Jesus' last Passover meal is the most distinctive section of all. John's first seven chapters are dominated by life, the next five chapters focus on light, but the rest of the book is mainly about love. John uses the word 'love' eight times in the first twelve chapters, and thirty times in the last nine.

Love dominates the 'Last Supper'. Throughout the meal, John describes the different ways in which God expresses his love for his friends, and he shows how those friends should respond to God's love with love for God and each other – for example, 13:1, 34; 14:21; 15:13; 16:27 and 17:26.

Only Luke uses the expression, 'filled with the Holy Spirit', and he looks to earth to show the Spirit as the special help that God gives to ordinary people. In contrast, John records Jesus' clearest teaching about the Spirit, and looks to heaven to reveal the Spirit issuing from the Father. It is John who identifies the Spirit as 'the Spirit of truth', describes him as the *Paraclete*, 'the Comforter', and introduces his work as teacher and witness.

Matthew, Mark and Luke focus on Jesus' human anguish and sorrow in his passion, and show him sharing his griefs with the apostles. John 14:27 looks at the same events from a different viewpoint and shows Jesus comforting his followers. It is the same in the garden: John 18:4–6 complements Luke's portrayal of the Son's struggle with the Father's will by presenting a peaceful Jesus who is in control of the situation.

After describing the resurrection, John brings his Gospel to a climax of belief, life and love in 20:27–31. Then, however, it is as though, having finished his conclusion, he feels compelled to add a postscript about love.

So this Gospel ends with another reminder that human work always ends in failure, another example of the Son bringing glory out of failure, another miracle in which the Son lavishly provides for people whose supply has been exhausted, and then it finally ends with three last questions about love.

Matthew's Gospel closes with the royal Son's declaration of absolute authority; Mark finishes by showing that the serving Son is still working with his disciples; Luke ends with the human Son's promise to send more help to his followers – and John concludes by showing that the divine Son is still looking for love.

Four Gospels, One Son

We have seen that the four Gospels offer distinctive portraits of the Son. Each Gospel contains special words, distinctive themes and unique insights, and each one begins and ends in a way which reflects its particular emphases.

There is, however, only one Jesus, only one Son, only one God, only one cross and only one 'gospel'. The four different Gospels do not lead to four different Sons; rather, they reveal the unique Son in inspired, complementary, overlapping ways. If we are to know the Son in the fullness of the biblical revelation, we need to know him, to worship him and to proclaim him in all these complementary ways – without over-emphasising one aspect or ignoring another.

Jesus is a unique being because only he is simultaneously both fully human and fully divine, only he is a king and a servant, a sinless human and the living God. Although each Gospel may concentrate on slightly different aspects of the Son's work and nature, together they present one gospel about one person.

Four 'hymns', one Son

After the careful portraits of the four Gospels, the rest of the New Testament focuses more on the consequences and implications of the Son's work than on detailed descriptions of his nature and mission. There are, however, two 'major' passages and two 'minor' passages which offer inspired and important summaries of his unique self.

Many scholars think that these passages were originally parts of hymns which were composed and used by the early church before being used in the New Testament. Whatever their origin, they contain valuable information about the Son which helps us to know him better.

PHILIPPIANS 2:5–11

Philippians
2:5–11 ☐

This famous 'hymn' is amazingly rich in statements about Christ Jesus the Son, and teaches much about his pre-existence, his incarnation and his exaltation.

The Son's pre-existence

Philippians 2:6 declares the Son's pre-existence, but some leaders disagree about its precise meaning. The Greek word *morphe*, 'form', is traditionally taken to mean 'essence'; and most church leaders have always believed this means that God's divine nature has always existed in the Son, and that the Son has always been fully equal with God.

Recently, however, a few people have suggested that *morphe* means 'condition' or 'image' rather than 'essence'. They argue that this is more consistent with Paul's teaching in 2 Corinthians 4:4 and Colossians 1:15, and that Jesus was, therefore, merely a representation of God – rather like Adam was an image of God. We will see, however, that 'image' in Colossians 1:15 means far more than representation, and that it involves the actual presence of God.

2 Corinthians 4:4 ☐

Colossians 1:15 ☐

It is not clear whether Philippians 2:6 means that Christ did not hold on to what he already possessed (equality with God), but willingly relinquished it; or whether it means that he resisted the temptation to grasp at what he did not yet possess (the dignity of kingship over creation), and was content to wait for this to be given to him. It may be that the verse is a deliberate ambiguity which points to both truths.

The Son's incarnation

Philippians 2:7–8 describes the Son's incarnation in terms of both the act of incarnation and the incarnate life. Again, many people disagree about the true meaning of verse 7.

Some suggest that the human Jesus could not have been divine if his equality with God had been laid aside; most argue that Jesus merely relinquished the public status of equality with God; while a few think that his 'emptying' should be understood simply as a revelation of divine self-effacement.

Paul's reference to 'a servant' in verse 7, and his description in verse 8, seem to refer to Isaiah's 'servant of God'. Just as verse 6 declares that Jesus was fully divine, so verse 7 states that he was fully human – that he was 'the Christ', 'the Anointed Man' whom we considered in Part One.

Although verse 8 suggests that Jesus' humanity is almost the exact opposite of his pre-existent divinity, Paul does not try to resolve the tension of the Son's dual nature: like all the other New Testament writers, he simply declares the mystery of Jesus' incarnation without attempting to explain or justify it.

The Son's exaltation

Philippians 2:9–11 proclaims the Son's exaltation, and suggests that this involves:

- *a divine act*

- *the gift of a unique name*

- *the worship of all people*

- *the universal acknowledgement of his sovereignty*

Most leaders believe that Jesus was exalted to an even higher status than his pre-existent, pre-incarnation status. Some, however, do not think that this can be possible, and they believe that verse 9 means Jesus was restored to his original status.

Verse 9 does not identify Jesus' new exalted name, but scholars have always assumed that Paul means the title, 'Lord' – which, as we have seen, was the name commonly used for Jesus after his resurrection.

Verses 10 and 11 underline the Son's exaltation by predicting universal worship in fulfilment of Isaiah 45:23. This is another proof that Jesus is just as divine as God himself – and the fact that the worship of Jesus glorifies God the Father shows that the Son is not an independent divine being.

COLOSSIANS 1:15–20

Whether or not this passage is an extract from an early hymn, it is a wonderful description of Christ which shows that the Son is:

- *superior to creation*

- *continuously active in creation*

- *the complete fullness of God*

Philippians
2:9–11 ☐

Isaiah 45:23 ☐

Colossians
1:15–20 ☐

The Son's supremacy

Paul claims in Colossians 1:15 that Jesus is the image of the invisible God, that he is the perfect revelation of God. The Bible always teaches that God is invisible, but Paul radically proclaims the visibility of the invisible through his perfect likeness in Christ. Paul is not suggesting that Jesus is a mere representation of God, but that the invisible has actually become visible in him.

Some people think that the phrase 'the first-born' means that Christ was a creature, but if Paul meant this he would not have stated in the following verse that the first-born was the creator of all things! This whole passage stresses the pre-existence and supremacy of the Son. Everything was made 'by him' and 'through him' and 'for him' – he is the source, the centre and the purpose of all creation.

The Son's sustenance

Hebrews 1:3 ☐

Colossians 1:17–18 echoes Hebrews 1:3 and shows that all things are held together in Christ: he is the principle of coherence in the universe, not an absent or disinterested creator, and he is the active, sustaining head of the church.

The Son's fullness

Colossians 2:9 ☐

Colossians 1:18–19 is Paul's climactic assertion about the Son. By declaring Christ's pre-eminence, Paul stresses Christ's uniqueness, but he then goes much further by linking 'pre-eminence' with 'fullness'. Colossians 2:9 shows that fullness means the total essence of God: quite simply, all that God is, is in Christ.

This is probably Paul's greatest and most important statement about the Son, and everything else that he writes about 'image' and 'form' must be understood in the light of Colossians 1:19 and 2:9.

Colossians 1:20 shows that the indwelling fullness of God in Christ has a functional purpose not just for humanity, but also for 'all things' – we consider this in *Reaching the Lost* and *Salvation by Grace*. This demonstrates that knowing the Son is deeply practical rather than idly theoretical. If we do not know him experientially as our personal reconciler, and if we do not know him experientially as the cosmic reconciler, all our theoretical knowledge is a useless waste of time.

OTHER HYMNS

1 Timothy 3:16 and Hebrews 1:3 are often thought to be extracts from hymns of the early church which celebrate the Son's unique life.

1 Timothy 3:16

1 Timothy 3:16 summarises the incarnation by stating that God was manifested in the flesh, by noting the close connection between the Son and the Spirit in the incarnate life (which we consider in Part Six) and by concluding that he was taken up in glory. This stress on the Son's glorious destiny is also seen in Philippians 2:11 and Hebrews 1:3.

Hebrews 1:3

Hebrews 1:3 sets out another high view of Christ which stresses the Son's relation to creation and to God. It uses two important Greek words to illustrate the Son's relation to God.

Apaugasma is often translated as 'brightness' or 'reflection', but it really means 'radiance': it suggests the dazzling brightness which streams from a brilliant light, and is used here to show (like Colossians 1:15 and John 1:14) that God's glory could be seen perfectly in his Son.

Charakter is usually translated as 'image' but it is a technical word which denotes the idea of an engraving tool, like the stamp on a seal, which bears the exact image of something so that it can reproduce it exactly. This shows both that there is an exact correspondence between the nature of the Son and the nature of the Father, and that the Son's incarnation is essentially functional.

Like Philippians 2:10–11, this verse also refers to the Son's exaltation by describing that he sat down 'at the right hand of the Majesty on high'. It shows that his exaltation followed on from his act of purging our sins – this is also implicit in the Philippians' reference to the Son's obedience to death on the cross.

The four hymns

The four 'Christological' hymns are important because they expand on many of the ideas which are implicit within the main New

1 Timothy 3:16 ☐
Hebrews 1:3 ☐

Philippians 2:11 ☐

Colossians 1:15 ☐
John 1:14 ☐

Philippians
    2:10–11 ☐

Testament titles or names of the Son, and because they make it undeniably clear that Jesus was both fully human and fully divine.

When we hold the hymns together, much as we hold the Gospels together, we see that they link the exaltation of the Son with his humiliation, and present an utterly unique being. Concepts like the 'no-snatching' of Philippians 2, the 'image' and 'fullness' of Colossians 1, and the divine 'radiance' of Hebrews 1 make it impossible to think that the Son was no more than just a human.

Although it is almost impossible for our human minds to grasp or explain the mystery of the Son's incarnation and his paradoxical dual nature, we must always try to hold together his exaltation and his humiliation, his glory and his lowliness, his majesty and his servant-hood, his authority and his meekness, his humanity and his divinity, his justice and his mercy. In fact, if we are not struggling to understand the fullness of the Son's unique nature, we probably do not know him very well.

PART FOUR

a unique life

The four Gospels describe a quite extraordinary life: Jesus' words, deeds, death and sinless perfection set him apart as a special person who was the centre of controversy in his own day, and who has been celebrated, revered and reviled for almost two thousand years.

Among all the different biblical reports of the Son's parables, miracles, compassion, righteous indignation, crucifixion, and so on, three events stand out as unique.

Throughout history, many other people have taught enduring stories and spiritual principles; several have worked genuine miracles; some have demonstrated deep compassion; and many have suffered terrible deaths. But nobody other than Jesus has experienced a virgin birth, or a resurrection from the dead, or an ascension to heaven.

Even though the New Testament presents these three supernatural episodes as actual historical events, they are a stumbling block to belief for many. People may believe that the Son was a good man, that he worked miracles, even that he was God – but they will not believe that he was born of a virgin, that he rose from the dead, and that he ascended on a cloud to heaven.

If we are to know the Son in the fullness of the scriptural revelation, we must know him personally – and proclaim him clearly – as the one whose life was framed by these three unique events.

THE VIRGIN BIRTH

We have seen that Matthew and Luke both describe a totally unusual birth, and that Luke devotes a considerable amount of space to the nativity stories. Their carefully researched stories are fundamental to our understanding of this unique event in the Son's life.

Luke

Luke 1:27–38 ☐

In 1:27–38, Luke describes Mary as a virgin, and reports the angel's announcement that she would conceive and bear a Son whose name should be Jesus, who would also be called 'the Son of the Most High', and who would be a permanent king in Israel: once again, this simple introduction to the Son combines the human and the divine.

When a bewildered Mary asks how this can happen because she is still a virgin, the angel does not go into any details about the mode of conception. He simply announces that the birth will not come about by the ordinary method of human reproduction, but by a totally unparalleled act of the Holy Spirit.

Luke 1:1–4 ☐
2:40 ☐
2:51–52 ☐

In 1:1–4, Doctor Luke declares that he is writing an orderly account of events which he has carefully investigated, checked with eye-witnesses, and considers to be 'certain'.

This first century medical expert then follows this with his descriptions of John's miraculous conception and the Son's supernatural conception – which he explains by the power of the Spirit. It is almost as though Luke is saying, 'I know that this is extraordinary, but trust me, I'm a doctor, I've checked it out, I've questioned the participants, I promise you, it happened just as I describe'.

By going on to describe Jesus' normal human growth, his obedience to his parents and his increase in wisdom – in 2:40 and 51–52 – Luke shows that the virgin birth does not deny Jesus' humanity; in this simple way he underlines that there is something both natural and supernatural about the Son.

We must accept that Luke presents Mary as a virgin and the virgin birth as an accepted fact. As even the most sceptical critics have been forced to recognise the complete accuracy of Luke's historical, political, geographical and archaeological details, it is now difficult to reject this part of his Gospel on any grounds other than blind, irrational prejudice.

Matthew

Although, as we have seen, Matthew describes Jesus' nativity from Joseph's point-of-view and largely ignores Mary, he does add to our understanding of the virgin birth. He explains, for example, that:

- *Jesus was born of Mary, rather than of Joseph and Mary* – 1:16

- *Mary was found with child of the Holy Spirit before she and Joseph 'came together'* – 1:18, 20

- *Joseph did not 'know' his wife until after she had given birth* – 1:25

- *the events fulfilled the Isaiah 7:14 prophecy of a virgin conceiving and bearing a Son, Emmanuel* – 1:23

Some people point out that *parthenos* literally means a 'young woman' rather than a 'virgin', but Matthew makes it very clear that Mary was a pure, unmarried woman, and so it is right to translate *parthenos* as 'virgin'.

Mark and John

We have already seen that Mark passes over the Son's birth and goes straight to his service, and that John sets out his heavenly origins.

Mark's only contribution to our understanding of Jesus' birth is in 6:3, where he records that the people of Nazareth referred to Jesus as 'Mary's son' – which was contrary to the normal Jewish practice.

Many people suggest that this points to Joseph's premature death, but John 6:42 refutes this. It is more likely that the people's comments in Mark 6:3 point to an unusual birth – just as they do in John 8:41.

Matthew 1:16 ☐
1:18–20 ☐
1:25 ☐
1:23 ☐

Mark 6:3 ☐

John 6:42 ☐
8:41 ☐

John 1:12–14 ☐

John's statement in 1:14, that the Word became flesh and dwelt among us, does not explain how this remarkable event happened, but it clearly requires some sort of mode by which a pre-existent being can become a human being.

Although John does not explain how Jesus was conceived and born, he does teach much about spiritual birth. Many leaders think that the location of John 1:12–13, immediately before 1:14, is significant, and that there is a link between the manner of Jesus' birth and the way that believers experience new birth.

Furthermore, John uses the same verb, *gennao*, (which refers to normal physical birth) throughout John 3 – where Jesus states that he came down from heaven and links this to being born of the Spirit.

1 John 2:29 ☐
3:9 ☐
4:7 ☐
5:4 ☐
5:18 ☐

Gennao is also used in 1 John 2:29; 3:9; 4:7; 5:4 and 18, and this suggests that there is some sort of parallel between the incarnation of Christ and the indwelling of Christ in those who are born of the Spirit.

Paul

Some scholars maintain that Paul did not believe in the virgin birth because he does not mention it in his epistles. An argument from silence, however, is always very weak; taken to its logical conclusion, this would mean that Paul did not believe in many of the Old Testament prophets and kings, and in vast chunks of the Scriptures.

Romans 1:3 ☐

Galatians 4:4 ☐

Philippians 2:7 ☐

Although there are no explicit references to Jesus' virgin birth in Paul's letters, there are several allusions. Most importantly, in Romans 1:3; Galatians 4:4 and Philippians 2:7, Paul does not use the normal verb *gennao* to describe the birth; instead, he uses the hard-to-translate verb *genomenos* which means 'come into being' more than 'born'.

The only logical explanation for this significant and consistent substitution is that Paul was seeking to differentiate the 'coming into being' of Jesus from normal human births.

The purpose of the virgin birth

A few believers argue that Jesus had to be born of a virgin to be free from original sin; but it was the Spirit's involvement in the conception which guaranteed Jesus' sinlessness, not Mary's sexual purity.

Others suggest that the idea of an incarnation demands a virgin birth, but God could surely have accomplished this in many different ways. All we can say for certain is that the virgin birth dramatically underlines the Son's uniqueness, and is entirely appropriate to the nature of the One who becomes human flesh even though he is equal with God.

There will always be a mystery about the incarnation and the virgin birth, for there is always a mystery about truly unique events. The Son's virgin birth may not be mentioned that frequently in the letters of the early church, but this may be because it was so deeply impressed in their consciousness that it was unnecessary to mention it repeatedly.

THE RESURRECTION

After Jesus' crucifixion, the disciples were a shattered band of people who were ready to return to their old homes and their old way of life. But something then happened which convinced them that Jesus was alive, and that they had a message which could transform the world.

Those sceptics who do not believe that the Son rose from the dead need to explain this dramatic turnaround, and the disciples' fearlessness in proclaiming the gospel – despite the terrible opposition that they faced. For Christians, the physical resurrection of Jesus is the obvious explanation for this sudden change in attitude and action.

In Acts 2:24, 36, the first Christian preachers announced that the one whom the Jews had crucified had been raised from the dead, and that God had made him both Lord and Christ. Something must have happened to produce this conviction, and the New Testament writers are unanimous in insisting that it was the physical resurrection of Jesus.

Acts 2:24 □
2:36 □

We consider all the different evidence for the resurrection in *Reaching the Lost*, and show how to answer the objections of those who reject the resurrection.

Acts 1:22 □
3:15 □
3:26 □
4:2 □
4:10 □
4:33 □
5:30 □
10:40 □
13:37 □
17:31 □
25:19 □

The resurrection was so important to the early church that, in Acts 1:22, only witnesses to the resurrection were considered as candidates for Judas' replacement. Then, throughout Acts, the resurrection was uppermost in the church's preaching and teaching: for example, 3:15, 26; 4:2, 10, 33; 5:30; 10:40; 13:37; 17:31 and 25:19.

The resurrection predicted

Matthew, Mark and Luke report that Jesus predicted his death three times, and that he linked this with the promise of a resurrection to follow after three days: we see this in Matthew 16:21; 17:22–23; 20:19; Mark 8:31; 9:31; 10:34; Luke 9:22 and 18:32–34.

The fact that Jesus made the prediction several times suggests he knew the disciples would not grasp the idea that easily. The disciples' problem seems to be that they had a wrong idea of Jesus' mission: Luke 24:21 shows that their hopes were fixed on a physical kingdom, and these were shattered by the crucifixion.

All the disciple's, except John, deserted Jesus and appear not to have been present at the cross. They had no faith in the spiritual purpose of Jesus' mission, and did not remember that he had predicted his death and a resurrection. As the Gospels show that the idea of a suffering Messiah was unacceptable not just to the Jews but also to the disciples, it is not surprising that they fled when Jesus was crucified.

The resurrection accomplished

The Bible never explains how God works creatively, because we do not know, and would never be able to understand, his divine processes. So the Gospel writers do not attempt to explain how God raised Jesus from the dead, they simply report what they saw:

- *the tomb was empty* – Matthew 28:1–15; Mark 16:4–11; Luke 24:2–4, 12; John 20:1–10

- *the risen Lord appeared to individual disciples, to small groups of them, and even to a crowd of five hundred* – Matthew 28:9, 16–20; Mark 16:9, 12, 14; Luke 24:13–53; John 20:14–29; 21:1–23; Acts 1:3, 4–8; 1 Corinthians 15:6

As we see in *Reaching the Lost*, those people who refuse to believe in the resurrection need to provide an alternative explanation for *both* these facts. Those who assert that the appearances were caused by hallucination cannot explain the empty tomb, and those who insist that the empty tomb was due to fraud cannot explain the risen appearances.

The Son's risen appearances confirmed his resurrection and provided a series of occasions when he could teach his disciples about the kingdom in the light of his resurrection.

The resurrection proclaimed

In 1 Corinthians 15:3–11, the apostle Paul says that he has 'received':

- *the fact of Christ's death*
- *the spiritual interpretation and application of his death*
- *the burial and resurrection*
- *the resurrection appearances*
- *scriptural attestation of the resurrection*

Paul lists the appearances to authenticate the resurrection, describes his own experience, and then applies this in his general proclamation and application of the resurrection in 15:12–58. In this passage, he asserts that the Christian faith would be futile if Christ were not risen. For Paul, the resurrection is at the centre of his faith and his thinking, as well as at the centre of his experience.

The resurrection permeates through Paul's teaching: for example, in his letter to the Romans, the resurrection:

- *testifies to Jesus' sonship – 1:4*
- *is linked to justification – 4:24–25*
- *is linked to salvation – 5:10*
- *is linked to baptism and entry to new life – 6:3*
- *is linked with the Spirit – 8:11*
- *is the guarantee of his intercession – 8:34*

Paul's other letters affirm and proclaim the resurrection – for example, Galatians 1:1; Ephesians 1:20; Philippians 3:10; Colossians 2:12; 3:1 and 1 Thessalonians 1:10. For him, the resurrection of the Son was an indisputable fact of history and fundamental to his preaching.

Paul, like us, had to learn about the resurrection from others, but Peter was an eye-witness, and – in 1 Peter 1:3, 21–22 – he shows its relationship with our new birth and our confidence in God. Peter was writing mainly to persecuted, suffering believers, and he promises them that their suffering will give way to the glory of the risen Christ: for Peter, the reality of the resurrection is the indispensable basis for hope. The apostle John was another eye-witness, and his book of Revelation centres on the risen Christ – we see this, for example, in 1:5, 17–18.

1 Corinthians 15:3–58	☐
Romans 1:4	☐
4:24–25	☐
5:10	☐
6:3	☐
8:11	☐
8:34	☐
Galatians 1:1	☐
Ephesians 1:20	☐
Philippians 3:10	☐
Colossians 2:12	☐
3:1	☐
1 Thessalonians 1:10	☐
1 Peter 1:3	☐
1:21–22	☐
Revelation 1:5	☐
1:17–18	☐

We see in *Salvation by Grace* that the resurrection is the proof of who Jesus is and what he achieves on the cross. When we think deeply, we should be able to see that the Son's dual nature depends on the resurrection being a real event.

Without the resurrection, the Son would have to be either a divine person who never really became human and who did not die, or a human person who was not divine, who died and did not rise. Only a resurrection guarantees the dual nature of Christ, and this is why it is vital to our understanding of the Son and central to our Christian faith.

We can understand the resurrection only as a supernatural act of God. Although Jesus claimed the power to take up his life after laying it down, in John 10:18, the New Testament never suggests that the resurrection was an independent act of Christ.

John 10:18 ☐

The power behind the resurrection was the power of God: it was a supreme display of divine power; it was the act which defeated death and checked corruption. By raising his Son from death to life, God provided humanity with a way from death to life – and this means that the resurrection is an essential part of God's plan for our salvation.

But this is not all there is to the resurrection, for it also expresses God's satisfaction with what Christ has done on the cross and vindicates his mission. If Christ had not been raised there would have been no visible proof that his death had accomplished anything.

On top of this, our assurance that Christ still cares for us today, and still intercedes for us, depends on his resurrection. His exalted position, his new name, his restored status, and his present activity, all depend upon his resurrection. As Paul states, without the Son's resurrection, our faith would be meaningless and our hope would be futile.

THE ASCENSION

The third unique event in the Son's earthly life was his ascension to heaven: this completed his resurrection and commenced his exaltation.

Mark 16:19 ☐

Luke 24:50–51 ☐

Mark 16:19 and Luke 24:50–51 record Jesus' departure from earth and reception into heaven, but they imply rather than record an ascension. Neither Matthew nor John mention Jesus' departure from earth, but John 3:13; 6:62 and 20:17 predict his ascension very clearly.

Acts 1:1–11 is the fullest account of the ascension. It shows that the Son continued to prove 'infallibly' the resurrection for forty days, and to teach the disciples about the kingdom. He then commanded them to stay in Jerusalem until they are baptised in the Holy Spirit. The ascension itself is described in verse 9.

Peter's first sermon, in Acts 2:14–36, shows how the disciples understood the ascension. In verses 33–34, he says that God has exalted Jesus at the right hand of God, and – as a result – the Spirit has been poured out. Peter then quotes from Psalm 110:1 to support what he says, for, unlike king David, Jesus has ascended to heaven.

Later, in Acts 3:21 and 5:31, Peter again describes the Son in terms of his ascended exaltation.

Paul affirms the ascension both directly and indirectly – as in Romans 10:6–7; Ephesians 1:20; 4:9–10; Colossians 3:1; 1 Thessalonians 1:10; 2 Thessalonians 1:7; Philippians 3:20 and 1 Timothy 3:16.

The book of Hebrews concentrates more on the ascended Christ than any other part of the Bible. Jesus is always presented as the one who is seated at the right hand of the Majesty on high, and we see his ascension, and its consequence, in 1:3; 4:14; 5:6; 6:20; 7:15–17, 21, 26; 8:1; 9:24; 10:12 and 12:2.

The ascension is also referred to in 1 Peter 3:18–22, and is the basic assumption behind all the heavenly activity recorded in Revelation.

When we think about Jesus' ascension, we can say that its importance lies more in its significance than in the event itself. For example, it was:

- *the completion of the resurrection* – as the resurrected conqueror of death, Jesus was the first fruits among his people; but as the ascended Son he carried forward that resurrection triumph to an exalted ministry on the part of his people.

- *the beginning of exaltation and enthronement* – Philippians 2:9–11 highlights the important present and future results of the ascension; the Son's present enthroned position is an enormous ground for our hope and encouragement.

John 3:13 ☐
6:62 ☐
20:17 ☐

Acts 1:1–11 ☐
2:14–36 ☐

Psalm 110:1 ☐

Acts 3:21 ☐
5:31 ☐

Romans 10:6–7 ☐

Ephesians 1:20 ☐
4:9–10 ☐

Colossians 3:1 ☐

1 Thessalonians
1:10 ☐

2 Thessalonians
1:7 ☐

Philippians 3:20 ☐

1 Timothy 3:16 ☐

Hebrews 1:3 ☐
4:14 ☐
5:6 ☐
6:20 ☐
7:15–17 ☐
7:21–26 ☐
8:1 ☐
9:24 ☐
10:12 ☐
12:2 ☐

1 Peter 3:18–22 ☐

Philippians
2:9–11 ☐

- *the commencement of heavenly intercession* – Christ's work of mediation between God and humanity depended on the mediator's entrance into heaven, just as the intercessory nature of the Jewish high priest depended on him gaining access to the holy of holies.

- *the fulfilment of the divine mission* – the Son's mission on earth which began with the virgin birth ended with the ascension: the incarnation was the fully divine Son becoming taking flesh and becoming fully human; the ascension was the fully divine, fully human Son returning to the Father.

  At the ascension, the Son took the evidence of human salvation (his 'yes' to God, his perfect obedience even to death on the cross) into the Father's presence. As the ascension was God's initiative, we can consider it to be God's seal on the whole mission of the Son.

Ephesians 4:8–10 ☐

- *the filling by Christ of all things* – Ephesians 4:8–10 presents this as the reason for the ascension. The filling of all things by Christ is the gathering up of all things into his own perfection, and this could be achieved only by the exalted Son.

John 7:39 ☐

- *the giving of the gift and gifts of the Holy Spirit* – In John 7:39, Jesus stated that the Spirit would be given only when he was glorified, and this is what Ephesians 4:8 describes on the basis of Psalm 68:18. Pentecost, therefore, was conditional upon the ascension, and the events of Acts 2:33 are the direct sequel of the ascension.

Psalm 68:18 ☐

Acts 2:33 ☐

- *the opening of access for believers* – as the Son gained access to the Father in the ascension, so he gained this right for all who are united to him. This means that Jesus' ascension is one of the great grounds for Christian hope and confidence.

- *the start of a new age* – the present age of the church is framed by two unique events: it began with the Son's ascension and it will end with his return – we see this link in Acts 1:11.

Acts 1:11 ☐

The present church age is the age of the risen and exalted Son, who is our mediator and intercessor; and our understanding of church history and current events must be shaped by our awareness of his exaltation-and-return – for, according to the Scriptures, the present is inextricably linked with the future. We consider this in Part Nine.

PART FIVE

a unique mission

In almost every book in this *Sword of the Spirit* series, we examine at least one aspect of the Son's unique mission. For example, in:

- *Effective Prayer*, we consider the part that prayer to the Father played in Jesus' earthly life

- *Knowing the Spirit*, we see how he depended entirely on the Holy Spirit for guidance and power in his ministry – and how he anoints us with the Spirit

- *The Rule of God*, we examine the Son's teaching about the kingdom of God

- *Living Faith*, we look at his faith, and consider the way that he used God's Word

- *Ministry in the Spirit*, we study the way that Jesus counselled people, cast out demons, healed the sick, and spoke with prophetic authority

- *Knowing the Father*, we think about his triune relationships within God and his ministerial partnership with the Father

- *Listening to God*, we see how the Son discerned what to say and to do in his earthly mission

- *Reaching the Lost*, we concentrate on his ministry of evangelism and see how he announced God's good news with words, deeds and a perfect life

- *Salvation by Grace*, we focus on Jesus' atoning death, and grasp that he died to conquer Satan, to save sinners, to reveal God's holy nature and to give God's new life to redeemed humanity

The Gospels

All four Gospels – from the opening verse of Matthew to the closing verse of John – are the Spirit-inspired, Spirit-directed record of the Son's mission. If, therefore, we sincerely want to know the Son, we must soak ourselves in the four Gospels; we must read them and re-read them, study them and meditate upon them, and allow God's Holy Spirit to reveal God's Personal Word through God's Written Word.

As we have seen, however, the four Gospels are not identical; instead, they each offer slightly different, but completely complementary, perspectives on the Son's unique mission.

For example, Matthew generally emphasises the truth that Jesus came to establish God's kingdom, and to conquer the evil powers of darkness: it underlines that the Son's mission involves *defeating Satan*.

Mark stresses the truth that Jesus came to be the suffering servant who bears the wrath of God against sin, and to reconcile man and women to God: it underlines that his mission involves *saving sinners*.

Luke seems to take pains to show that Jesus came to be the pattern for every man and woman; in his daily death to self and the desires of the flesh, he came to show humanity how to live and die: it underlines that the Son's mission involves *living the perfect human life*.

And John reveals that Jesus came to show the world what God is like, to reveal and reproduce the Father's nature, to be a perfect revelation of the living God: it underlines that his mission involves *giving God's own new life* to humanity.

Of course, when we look closely at the Gospels, we see every facet of Jesus' mission in every Gospel – it is just that each writer tends to highlight a different aspect of the mission. And they all show that Jesus fulfilled every facet of his mission in both his life *and* his death.

In this chapter, we consider the mission of the Son through his life; and, in Part Eight, we examine the Gospel accounts of his death. His mission through his death, however, is so important and vast that we have allocated one full book in this series, *Salvation by Grace*, to its study. As we say in the introduction to this book, we cannot know the Son in the fullness of the biblical revelation without working through both *Knowing the Son* and *Salvation by Grace*.

THE SON'S BAPTISM

The Son's daring mission to rescue and redeem fallen humanity began with his baptism and temptation, and this is recorded in Matthew 3:13–4:11; Mark 1:9–13; Luke 3:21–22; 4:1–14; and John 1:29–36.

Matthew 3:13–4:11 ☐

Mark 1:9–13 ☐

Luke 3:21–22 ☐
4:1–14 ☐

John 1:29–36 ☐

When we examine these accounts, we can look at the beginning of Jesus' mission from several different viewpoints. We can see, for example, that the Son came to the Jordan to obey the Father and to submit to his will; and that then, after submitting and obeying, he went forward in authority to rule over Satan.

If, however, we look at the baptism from another perspective, we can *also* see that Jesus came to the Jordan willing to take a lowly position and to accept ministry from his human cousin. The Son then went away into the wilderness to be looked after by angels, to be with wild animals, and to prepare for sacrificial service.

But if we look at the same event from yet another angle, we can say that Jesus *also* came to the Jordan to be anointed with the Holy Spirit. The Son left behind his family, friends, job, security and possessions, and put himself unconditionally at the disposal of the Father. Then, after his anointing with the Spirit, he followed the Spirit into the desert, ready to lead men and women and to call them to follow him.

Finally, we can *also* see that Jesus came to the Jordan as 'the Lamb of God' to show people what God is really like. As 'the Lamb', the Son went down into the water to symbolise death, and he came up from the water to begin offering new 'resurrection' life to humanity.

Whenever we think about (or proclaim) any aspect of the Son's mission, we must try to remember these complementary perspectives – because all are true and all are biblical. If we repeatedly overlook one emphasis, or continually stress another, we will not know the Son (or make him known to others) in the fullness of the biblical revelation.

Of course, in any one sermon or situation, it will usually be right to stress one perspective more than another; but we must appreciate the full biblical picture of the Son's unique mission if we are to know and proclaim the Son as he has been revealed to us in the Word.

The prophetic phases of the baptism

There seem to be several phases in the accounts of Jesus' baptism.

- *he goes down into the water*

- *he rises up from the water*

- *he stands praying*

- *the heavens open and the Spirit descends onto him*

This prophetic sequence of 'death', 'resurrection', 'prayer' and 'anointing with the Spirit' runs through Jesus' mission on earth. For example, we can say that the Son died every day to self; that he always lived the victorious risen life; that he always prepared for everything in prayer; and that he was always reassured, directed and empowered by the Holy Spirit for every aspect of his ministry.

This sequence of prophetic phases was then perfectly fulfilled by the Son's death on the cross, by his resurrection from the dead, by his prayers for his disciples and for the Spirit to come, and by the way that he poured out the Spirit at Pentecost to equip the church for mission.

Once again, it is easy to focus on only one of these 'phases', and to concentrate on applying just one phase in believers' lives today. While it is clearly right, for example, to stress the importance of prayer, it is not right to suggest that prayer is everything. Jesus did prepare for everything in prayer; but he did not only pray to the Father, for he also got on with the task that the Father had given him.

Equally, while it is plainly correct to underline the vital importance of the Spirit's anointing, it is not right to give the impression that nothing else matters. Jesus did depend on the Spirit's anointing, enabling and fellowship; but he also died to self, prayed to the Father, triumphed over Satan, served other people, and so on.

Although, today, we do need to stress the importance of dying to self, we should not imply that this is the 'be-all and end-all' of Christian discipleship. Jesus did die daily to self, he did conquer every fleshly urge, he did overcome every demonic temptation; but his life was never negative, for he also lived an abundant, anointed, prayerful, 'resurrected' life which was full of joy and vitality.

These 'prophetic phases' of the Son's baptism are all biblical emphases, and are all firmly rooted in the Son's mission; but they are not independent or exclusive emphases. In fact, we can say that the Son's mission was unique partly because so many complementary aspects were always held together in perfect union.

The symbolism of the Son's baptism

When we think about each of these prophetic phases symbolically, we can say that his descent into the water represents, for example,

- *judgement and repentance*

- *bearing the sins of the world*

- *dedicating everything to God*

- *a grain of wheat going into the ground to reproduce itself*

These symbolic interpretations are equally valid, but none is valid if it is taken in isolation. We need every biblical perspective on the Son's unique mission to understand and interpret it correctly and completely.

When we look at the other phases of the baptism, we can say that the Son's rising from the water symbolises, for example:

- *his resurrection authority*

- *his cleanliness*

- *his public ministry*

- *a new shoot which will reproduce itself many times over*

We can also say that Jesus stood praying for:

- *his mind and body and spirit to be entirely under God's authority*

- *his sacrifice to be effective in his followers' lives*

- *that he would live his life faultlessly and accomplish everything God had purposed for him*

- *God to glorify himself and make the Son fruitful*

And we can also understand the pouring out of the Spirit as:

- *an empowerment with authority for the Son's confrontation with evil spirits and disease*

- *an equipping for the Son's dove-like sacrifice and service*

- *a gift of vital assurance*

- *the indispensable resource for radiating God's glory and love*

It should be obvious that all these sets of symbolic interpretations are equally true, but that none is the whole truth on its own. We must recognise that Satan causes more confusion and division within the church through tempting believers to over-emphasise or overlook one particular truth than through deceiving them with outright falsehood.

It is very difficult for any one person or congregation to know and proclaim the full truth about the full nature and mission of Jesus – which is why there are four gospels and not one. However, like each Gospel, we should stand with those who complement our emphasis as well as with those who share our emphasis.

A multi-faceted mission

The truth is that the Son's baptism, the starting point of his mission, symbolised and revealed a unique 'multi-faceted' mission, which Jesus demonstrated in his life and fulfilled in his death.

When we take an overview of the different Gospel strands and emphases, we can say that the Father sent the Son to earth (and that the Son willingly came) with a mission to break the power of evil.

Satan had taken authority on earth and the whole world was under his sway, so the Son came into the world to establish the kingdom of heaven, to disarm the evil powers of darkness, and to triumph decisively over them. He came to preach a message of repentance, to teach people the consequence of disobedience, and to give them clear guidelines for living in the kingdom of God.

However, we can *also* say that the Father sent the Son with a mission to seek and save the lost. He came to save needy people who were powerless to save themselves. At great personal sacrifice, the Son came to make atonement for sin, to be the substitute for each member of humanity, and to bear the just wrath of God against sin.

We can *also* say that the Father sent the Son (and the Son willingly came) to demonstrate a human life of perfect consecration and holiness. He came to be the pattern and example for all men and women, of all ages and every race. In the way that he lived and died, he came to show human beings how they were meant to live and die.

And we can *also* say that the Father sent the Son to show the world what God is like. So it was the Son's mission to reveal the glorious Father in all his majesty, to be God's living Word, to be a unique and complete public revelation of the invisible God.

THE SON'S MISSION STATEMENT

Jesus revealed much more about of his unique, multi-faceted mission when he addressed the Nazareth synagogue after leaving the wilderness. His words in Luke 4:18–19 are particularly illuminating, and are among the Son's most important statements: we can think of this passage as his 'mission statement'.

Luke 4:18–19 ☐

In Luke 4:18–19, Jesus first explains that the purpose of his anointing with the Holy Spirit at his baptism in the Jordan is 'preaching or spreading good news to the poor or hurting' – we examine this closely in *Reaching the Lost*.

He then goes on to offer five examples of what 'evangelising the hurting' means in practice: this is probably the Son's clearest definition of his mission. We can say that, according to Jesus, his unique mission involves:

- *healing the broken-hearted*

- *liberating the captives*

- *restoring sight to the blind*

- *releasing the oppressed*

- *proclaiming God's message of freedom and favour*

The Son was not sent from the Father, and anointed with the Spirit, just with a mission of preaching. Rather, he came to reveal God through words, deeds and a perfect life; and he came to do this for the poor – the Greek word *ptochos* means 'the afflicted' or 'the hurting'.

Luke 7:18–22 ☐

The idea of a multi-faceted mission is repeated in Luke 7:18–22. John wanted to know whether Jesus was the long-expected Messiah, and sent two disciples to check. Verse 21 describes Jesus' response to their questions; and verse 22 records his message to John: the disciples had to report what they had *seen* and *heard* – that the blind could see, the lame could walk, the lepers were healed, the deaf could hear, the dead were raised, and the poor were hearing the good news.

Luke 8:1–56 ☐

This idea is underlined in Luke 8. Verse 1 describes the Son as *kerusson* and *euangelizmenos*, 'preaching and bringing the glad tidings', to every city and village in the area. Verses 2–56 then illustrate verse 1, and show that Jesus' mission included:

- *preaching and answering questions* – verse 4–18
- *bringing peace* – verse 22–25
- *liberating captives* – verse 26–39
- *healing the sick* – verse 43–48
- *raising the dead* – verse 49–56

It is the same in the other Gospels. Mark, for example, begins his account of the Son's mission by recording one day in his life. Verses 21–34 show that, in a typical day, Jesus:

Mark 1:21–34 ☐

- *preached in the synagogue* – verse 21–22
- *delivered a captive* – verse 23–26
- *healed the sick* – verse 29–31, 34
- *cast out demons* – verse 34

In every Gospel, we see that the Son ministered to vast crowds, small groups and large numbers of hurting individuals. Although the Son's mission was always multi-faceted, the people of his day would have been aware of three primary activities. They saw that he released people from the grip of evil; that he healed their diseases; and that he taught them about God's kingdom. In doing all this, the Son also revealed to them the love and glory of the living God.

1.   THE SON BREAKS EVIL'S POWER

We see in *The Rule of God* that God's righteous kingdom arrived in-and-with Jesus. Although the Son's decisive victory over Satan was achieved in his death on the cross, the early rounds were won in his perfect submission to his Father throughout his earthly life *and* in the mighty works which demonstrated his unique anointing and authority.

As soon as Jesus was born, Satan recognised him as his future conqueror and started to attempt to defeat him. He attacked Jesus through:

- *the slaughter of the Bethlehem children* – Matthew 2:13–18

- *the wilderness temptations* – Matthew 4:1–11

- *the Nazareth congregation's attempts on his life* – Luke 4:28–29

- *the crowds desire to make him a political ruler* – John 6:15

- *Peter's opposition to the way of the cross* – Matthew 16:21–23

- *Judas' betrayal* – Luke 22:1–6; John 13:27

But Jesus was determined to fulfil what had been foretold. He announced that God's kingdom had come in-and-through him, and that his mighty works were the visible proof of its coming.

In the Gospels, we see God's kingdom advancing and Satan's kingdom retreating as demons are cast out, diseases are healed and nature is calmed – for example, Matthew 4:23; Mark 1:24; 4:39.

Luke 9:1–6 and 10:1–24 report that Jesus sent out over eighty disciples to announce the kingdom's arrival by preaching, healing and casting out demons. When they returned, he told them that he had seen Satan fall from heaven as a result of their activities.

Mark 3:27 and Luke 11:21–22 seem to summarise Jesus' understanding of his struggles with Satan before the cross. The devil may have been a very strong man, but a stronger man had come – and he would bind and overpower the strong man and plunder his house.

1 John 3:8 stresses that the Son came to undo what Satan had done in corrupting God's creation, especially through sin: it was his mission to bring deliverance to humanity. And Matthew 12:28 shows that breaking the power of evil was at the heart of Jesus' kingdom message.

Matthew 2:13–18 ☐
4:1–11 ☐

Luke 4:28–29 ☐

John 6:15 ☐

Matthew
16:21–23 ☐

Luke 22:1–6 ☐

John 13:27 ☐

Matthew 4:23 ☐

Mark 1:24 ☐
4:39 ☐

Luke 9:1–6 ☐
10:1–24 ☐

Mark 3:27 ☐

Luke 11:21–22 ☐

1 John 3:8 ☐

Matthew 12:28 ☐

In his life, his words and his deeds, the Son broke the power of evil; and this aspect of his mission reached its climax on the cross – the supreme act of deliverance. Hebrews 2:14–15 describes how Jesus defeated Satan and the power of death, and released those who were held captive.

Although the full breaking of evil's power did not take place until the cross, we must take care that we do not limit the Son's defeat of Satan to the cross – as this ignores an important aspect of his mission. The Gospels show that, long before the cross, Jesus consistently released people from the power of evil forces. We see this, for example, in these incidents:

- *the Capernaum demoniac* – Mark 1:21–28; Luke 4:31–37

- *Peter's mother-in-law* – Matthew 8:14–15; Mark 1:29–31; Luke 4:38–39

- *the blind and dumb demoniac* – Luke 11:14–22

- *the Gadarene demoniacs* – Matthew 8:28; Mark 5:1–20; Luke 8:26–39

- *the Canaanite's daughter* – Matthew 15:21–28; Mark 7:24–30

- *the epileptic demoniac* – Matthew 17:14–21; Mark 9:14–29; Luke 9:37–43

- *the crippled woman* – Luke 13:10–17

- *the dumb demoniac* – Matthew 9:32–34

The Gospels also contain these statements about the Son's mission to break the power of evil: Matthew 4:24; 8:16; Mark 1:32–34, 39; 3:11; 6:13; Luke 4:41; 6:18; 7:21 and 11:24–26. These incidents and statements suggest several practical principles about the Son's mission to break the power of evil in the lives of enslaved men and women.

- *he delivered people who were brought to his attention*

The Gospels indicate that, when Jesus was ministering, he released all those who were brought to him needing help. He cast out demons when he was asked by a representative of the sufferer, when a demon reacted to his presence, and when he was led to a sufferer by the Spirit.

- *he asked few questions*

Once Jesus had established that the sufferer needed to have a demon cast out, he did not attempt to establish the cause – only to expel the demon. In fact, the Gospels describe Jesus questioning only two sufferers during casting out ministry.

- *he spoke directly to the demon*

The Son's authoritative words were directed at the demon controlling or influencing the person rather than at the person. Jesus did not ignore the sufferer, and his ministry was within the context of offering spiritual support and direction to the person, but – during the time of ministry – Jesus spoke to the demon.

The Gospels record that Jesus 'bound', 'muzzled' and 'rebuked' demons, that he ordered them to 'come out', asked them their names when necessary, and commanded them not to return.

- *he made no distinction between sufferers*

The Gospels do not show the Son making a distinction between matters like 'oppression', 'possession', 'depression', 'infestation', 'attack', 'affliction', and so on. Instead, they use one Greek word, *daimonizomai*, to describe almost everyone who needed release.

- *he distinguished casting out demons from healing*

Matthew 8:16; Mark 1:32–34; Luke 4:40–41; 6:18 and 7:21 distinguish between healing and expelling demons. And Matthew 4:24 makes a distinction between *daimonizomai* and *seleniazomai* – between demonisation needing deliverance and epilepsy needing healing.

Matthew 8:16 ☐
Mark 1:32–34 ☐
Luke 4:40–41 ☐
6:18 ☐
7:21 ☐
Matthew 4:24 ☐

- *he relied on the Spirit*

The Son claimed to eject demons through the Spirit of God. His ministry was a personal confrontation between the One who was full of the Holy Spirit and an unclean spirit.

- *he terrified demons*

The Gospels show that, even before their defeat at Calvary, demons were terrified of Jesus. Instead of remaining silent in his presence, they were so afraid that they shrieked and exposed themselves. They always had to obey Jesus. When he said 'Come out,' they came out; even if their exits were noisy and violent.

- *he impressed people*

The Gospels show that this aspect of the Son's mission made a great impact. Mark 1:21–28 reports astonishment and a spreading reputation; Luke 9:43 comments that the crowds were awe-struck by the greatness of God; and Luke 8:37 describes panic and an urgent request for Jesus to leave the area. However, Matthew 9:34; 12:24; Mark 3:22; Luke 11:15; John 7:20; 8:48 and 10:20 record a rather different reaction.

2. THE SON HEALS THE SICK

Like the other facets of his unique mission, the Son's healing activity can be viewed from several scriptural perspectives.

We can think of healing as part of the Son's calling to break the power of evil, and can stress that he ruled over disease much as he ruled over demons – because of his royal authority.

But we can *also* think of healing as part of the Son's calling to serve needy humanity, and can stress that people are made whole through the self-sacrifice of his wounds and though his atoning blood.

We can *also* think of healing as part of the Son's prophetic ministry, and can stress that he healed people because he was the Christ who was filled with the Spirit like the healing prophets of old.

And we can *also* think of healing as a wonderful revelation of *Yahweh Rapha*, 'the Lord who heals', and can stress that Jesus healed the sick because he was the healing God present in person.

Once again, we must hold these complementary perspectives together if we are to understand the Son's mission in its perfect fullness.

When Jesus returned to his local synagogue in Nazareth to introduce himself as the fulfilment of Isaiah 61:1–2, he announced that he had been anointed with the Spirit – and *therefore* was now healing the broken-hearted and giving new sight to the blind. From this point on, the Gospels show that healing was a major and distinguishing feature of the Son's mission on earth. Quite simply, whenever we overlook or understate the Son's healing activity, we misrepresent his unique mission to the world.

The Son's healing mission

The Gospels offer these illustrations of Jesus' healing mission:

- *the nobleman's son at Capernaum* – John 4:43–54

- *Jairus' daughter* – Matthew 9:18–26; Mark 5:21–43; Luke 8:40–56

- *the woman with the issue of blood* – Matthew 9:20–22; Mark 5:25–34; Luke 8:43–48

- *two blind men* – Matthew 9:27–31

- *the paralysed man let down through the roof* – Matthew 9:1–8; Mark 2:2–12; Luke 5:17–26

- *a leper* – Matthew 8:1–4; Mark 1:40–45; Luke 5:12–14

- *the centurion's servant* – Matthew 8:5–13; Luke 7:1–10

- *Peter's mother-in-law* – Matthew 8:14–15; Mark 1:29–31; Luke 4:38–39

- *the widow of Nain's son* – Luke 7:11–17

- *the lame man at the pool of Bethesda* – John 5:1–18

- *the man born blind* – John 9:1–41

- *the man with the withered hand* – Matthew 12:9–14; Mark 3:1–6; Luke 6:6–11

- *the woman bent double* – Luke 13:10–17

- *the man with dropsy* – Luke 14:1–6

- *the ten lepers* – Luke 17:11–19

- *the deaf and dumb man* – Mark 7:31–37

- *the blind man of Bethsaida* – Mark 8:22–26

- *Lazarus* – John 11:1–44

- *the blind men of Jericho* – Matthew 20:29–34; Luke 18:35–43

- *the high priest's servant* – Luke 22:47–51

The Gospels also record these statements about Jesus' healing ministry: Matthew 4:23–25; 8:16–17; 9:35; 11:4–5; 12:15–1614:14, 34–36; 15:30–31; 19:2; 21:14; Mark 1:32–34; 3:10–12; 6:55–56; Luke 4:40; 5:15–16; 6:17–19; 7:21–22; 8:2; 9:11 and John 6:2.

These passages suggest some practical principles about the Son's mission to heal the sick and hurting.

John 4:43–54 ☐
Matthew 9:18–26 ☐
Mark 5:25–34 ☐
Matthew 9:27–31 ☐
Luke 5:17–26 ☐
Matthew 8:1–4 ☐
Luke 7:1–10 ☐
Mark 1:29–31 ☐
Luke 7:11–17 ☐
John 5:1–18 ☐
John 9:1–41 ☐
Mark 3:1–6 ☐
Luke 13:10–17 ☐
Luke 14:1–6 ☐
Luke 17:11–19 ☐
Mark 7:31–37 ☐
Mark 8:22–26 ☐
John 11:1–44 ☐
Matthew 20:29–34 ☐
Luke 22:47–51 ☐
Matthew 4:23–25 ☐
    8:16–17 ☐
    9:35 ☐
    11:4–5 ☐
    12:15–16 ☐
    14:14 ☐
    14:34–36 ☐
    15:30–31 ☐
    19:2 ☐
    21:14 ☐
Mark 1:32–34 ☐
    3:10–12 ☐
    6:55–56 ☐
Luke 4:40 ☐
    5:15–16 ☐
    6:17–19 ☐
    7:21–22 ☐
    8:2 ☐
    9:11 ☐
John 6:2 ☐

• *he healed ordinary people*

The Gospels describe Jesus healing mainly ordinary men and women: they offer nineteen examples of him healing 'social outcasts' and eleven examples of him healing ordinary people with terrible afflictions.

• *he healed serious matters*

The Son concentrated on healing people whose sickness had caused isolation, loneliness, unemployment, or had persisted for a long time.

• *he healed on the streets*

Jesus sometimes healed crowds at informal gatherings, but he more usually went to individual people and healed them where they were. He healed people on journeys, in homes, in gardens, at meals, a funeral, a graveyard, a pool, and regular services in the synagogue.

• *he responded to people and the Spirit*

The Son's healing ministry was initiated either in response to people saying, 'Please heal me' or 'Please heal my friend', or to the Holy Spirit ordering him to, 'Go heal that person'.

Jesus did not heal all the sick in Israel, but he was always certain of the Father's willingness to heal; he healed all who came asking for healing; and he healed all who were identified to him by the Spirit.

• *he ministered with commands and touch*

When ministering, Jesus did not ask God to heal people; instead, he was so aware of God's will and timing that either he touched people to signify God's healing or he spoke a prophetic command of healing.

• *he impressed people*

The Gospels show that, through the Son's healing ministry, people were converted, the news of the kingdom spread, and the crowds admired Jesus. At times, however, the response was persecution, argument, even plots of destruction – in fact, the chief priests seized the Son while their servant's severed ear was being healed.

• *he involved others in his mission*

Jesus trained over eighty disciples to continue his healing mission after his ascension. First, he ensured that they were with him when he healed; then he invested them with his authority to cure the sick and sent them out in pairs to heal and preach the good news.

3. THE SON PROCLAIMS THE KINGDOM

Mark 1:14–15 shows that Jesus began his mission by announcing that the kingdom of God was at hand. He repeated this claim in Matthew 12:28 and Luke 11:20, and evidenced it by casting out demons. In fact, all Jesus' miraculous activity proved that God's kingdom had come.

Mark 1:14–15 ☐

Matthew 12:28 ☐

Luke 11:20 ☐

But as well as teaching that the kingdom had come, Jesus also taught that the kingdom was 'not yet'. We see this, for example, in Matthew 5:1–10; 6:10; 7:21–22; 8:11; 13:42–43; 16:27–28; 20:21; 26:29; Mark 9:1; 10:37; 14:25; Luke 13:28–29 and 22:18. We consider the 'now and not yet' dynamic of the kingdom in *The Rule of God*.

Matthew 5:1–10 ☐
6:10 ☐
7:21–22 ☐
8:11 ☐
13:42–43 ☐
16:27–28 ☐
20:21 ☐
26:29 ☐

Mark 9:1 ☐
10:37 ☐
14:25 ☐

Luke 13:28–29 ☐
22:18 ☐

In his teaching, the Son showed that the kingdom:

- *belongs to God*

- *is dynamic and powerful*

- *is established personally by the Son*

- *means salvation*

Jesus' often used parables to teach the people about the kingdom of God. When we take an overview of his parables, we can see that several themes run through them.

Matthew 13:1–52 ☐

- *the kingdom will continue to grow*

Growth occurs in several 'parables of the kingdom' which are recorded in Matthew 13 – for example, the Sower (1–23), the Tares (24–30) and the Mustard Seed (31–32).

- *the kingdom is hidden*

The Leaven or Yeast (33) shows that outstanding results are achieved by inconspicuous methods. This is the opposite of worldly thinking.

- *the kingdom is precious*

The Treasure (44) and the Pearl (45–46) point to the incomparable value of the kingdom – yet its value is not appreciated or sought by all.

- *the kingdom is a mystery*

The Dragnet (47–52) and the Tares (24–30) show that the righteous and the unrighteous stay mixed in the world until the last day. No attempt must be made to separate them before the end, because only the king can be trusted to judge correctly.

- *the kingdom is international*

Matthew
21:33–46 ☐

The Vineyard, in Matthew 21:33–46, implies that the kingdom is not only for Jews but also for people of other nations.

- *the kingdom demands repentance and obedience*

Matthew
21:28–32 ☐

The Two Sons, Matthew 21:28–32, shows the need for repentance and obedience. Tax collectors will enter the kingdom before religious leaders – if they fulfil the conditions of entry and the leaders do not.

- *the kingdom is important*

Matthew 25:1–13 ☐
22:1–14 ☐

The Virgins, Matthew 25:1–13, and the Marriage Feast, Matthew 22:1–14, warn against ignoring the kingdom. Although the warnings are set in the future, their challenge is immediate.

- *the kingdom will be opposed*

The Sower and the Tares suggest that the Kingdom is opposed at every turn. Although growth is certain, it will always be resisted.

The Son's kingdom message

Mark 1:14–15 ☐

After John had been imprisoned, Jesus preached more widely. Mark 1:14–15 records his message that 'the time is fulfilled, and the kingdom of God is at hand. Repent and believe the gospel'.

Matthew 3:1–2 ☐
4:17 ☐

Matthew 3:1–2 and 4:17 describe much the same message at the start of the Son's mission. This suggests that the coming of the kingdom was not only an event which had to be proclaimed, it was also a challenge to which people had to respond.

For the Son, the coming of the kingdom was such a significant event that people had to change the way they thought and the way they behaved. He announced the kingdom's arrival in clear terms.

1. *The time has come. The age of God's personal rule is beginning.*

2. *You are called to make a radical, personal response to the presence of God's personal rule.*

3. *God requires you to surrender to his personal rule. You must repent and believe.*

Jesus always made it plain that 'repent' was the primary call of the kingdom. We see this, for example, in Matthew 4:17; Mark 6:12; Luke 5:32; 13:3–5; 15:7, 10 and 24:47.

Metanoeo is the Greek verb for 'to repent', and literally means 'to change your mind'. This suggests that the Son's proclamation of kingdom repentance means a radical transformation of thought, attitude, outlook and direction. It means a mental revolution about God, his nature and rule, Jesus, sin, holiness and ourselves. We consider this fully in *The Rule of God*.

The Son made it clear that repentance was an essential requirement for his followers. In fact, until people change their mind about their sin and God's holiness, they are not aware that they need to be saved.

Once we grasp that 'repent' means 'change your mind', it becomes clear why the Son links 'belief' with 'repentance'. It is obvious that every change of mind must involve believing something new. Jesus' call to believe the gospel simply means believing in Jesus himself. His listeners were expected to commit themselves to *all* that he stood for – to every aspect of his multi-faceted mission.

When Jesus proclaimed the kingdom, he was calling people to establish a new relationship with him which was characterised by repentance and belief. Mark 1:15–20 shows how Jesus moved from announcing the kingdom's arrival, through calling people to repent and believe, to calling people to follow him personally. Matthew 4:17–22 records the same progression. This shows that the Son's unique mission involved calling people to become his personal disciples.

The Gospels offer many different examples of the Son's proclamation of kingdom discipleship. They show that:

- *kingdom discipleship is personal*

The Son did not call people to follow a set of ideas or rules but to follow *him*; in the same way, in Matthew 11:29 he called people to learn from *him* personally and not from the Law or a book.

- *kingdom discipleship is urgent*

The Gospels record many stories about people whom Jesus called to become disciples. They had to respond when he called them, even if this meant disruption for them and the people around them. We see this, for example, in Matthew 4:18–22; 9:9; Matthew 19:21; Luke 9:59

Matthew 4:17 ☐

Mark 6:12 ☐

Luke 5:32 ☐
　　13:3–5 ☐
　　15:7, 10 ☐
　　24:47 ☐

Mark 1:15–20 ☐

Matthew 4:17–22 ☐

Matthew
　　11:28–30 ☐

Matthew 4:18–22 ☐
　　9:9 ☐
　　19:21 ☐

Luke 9:59 ☐

John 1:43 ☐

and John 1:43. Some immediately followed Jesus, but others made excuses. The Son's call may be compelling but it is never compulsory.

- *kingdom discipleship is absolute*

Mark 10:33 ☐

Luke 9:62 ☐

John 8:31–32 ☐

The Son called people to forsake all and follow him fully. We see this, for example, in Mark 10:33; Luke 9:62 and John 8:31–32. Becoming a disciple of Jesus is not merely an emotional response or mental assent to his teaching – it is a permanent decision to follow the Son, to learn from him, to obey him, to keep close to him at all times.

- *kingdom discipleship is costly*

Matthew 6:33 ☐

16:13–33 ☐

Mark 8:34 ☐

Luke 5:1–11 ☐

9:23 ☐

12:31–34 ☐

Jesus never suggested that following him would easy: time and again he spelt out the cost of commitment, the cost of discipleship. We see this, for example, in Matthew 6:33; 16:13–33; Mark 8:34; Luke 5:1–11; 9:23 and 12:31–34.

THE PURPOSE OF HIS UNIQUE MISSION

There is an obvious progression in the Son's kingdom message. First, he calls people to change the way that they think about God; next, he calls them to believe in him, to rely on him and trust him completely; then, he calls them to follow him closely and become his disciples.

But this is not the end. We are not called only to follow the Son, we are also called to become like him. His mission is not just to collect converts and to make disciples, it is also to transform them into his personal likeness.

The Gospels stress five important ways in which the Son wants his disciples to become more like him.

- *love like him*

John 13:34–35 ☐

In John 13:34–35, the Son taught his disciples a new commandment which would prove to 'all' that they were his disciples.

- *give like him*

John 15:13–14 ☐

In John 15:13–14, Jesus explained exactly what he meant by loving. It is sacrificial giving; it is laying down our lives for our friends.

- *serve like him*

In Mark 10:42–45, Jesus showed his disciples that they were to serve in an entirely different way to the world.

Mark 10:42–45 ☐

- *work like him*

In John 14:12, Jesus revealed to his disciples that they should work like him. Many people assume the Jesus was referring to casting out demons and healing the sick. As we have seen, these are important elements of the Son's mission; but we must recognise that this verse is set in the same sacrificial context as his commands to give, to love and to serve. If we believe in the Son we should expect to live like the Son – this included mighty miracles, but it is all characterised by service.

John 14:12 ☐

- *go like him*

John 20:19–22 records Jesus' first words to his disciples after his resurrection, and verse 21 is his final call to them to be like him.

John 20:19–22 ☐

In Part Seven, we will see how John's Gospel stresses that the Son is so under the personal rule of God that he says nothing of his own, does nothing of his own and goes nowhere on his own initiative. He speaks what the Father says. He does what the Father does. He goes where the Father sends. And he does all this in the power of the Spirit.

In the same way, Jesus sends his disciples as he has been sent – to go into the world as he has goes, to submit to the Father as he submits, to rely on the Spirit as he relies, to share with him in his unique mission.

We have stressed that it is important to understand the Son's unique, multi-faceted mission correctly; now we should begin to grasp why it is important: it is because he is calling us to share with him in his unique mission, to pass on his message of reconciliation, to apply his victory over evil, to glorify the living God, to heal the sick, and to preach the good news of the kingdom to the hurting people around us.

PART SIX

the son and the spirit

We have seen that, in their complementary ways, all four Gospels make it plain that a new age dawned with the coming of the Son to earth: the age of God's kingdom, the age of the Messiah; the age of the widespread availability of the Holy Spirit.

The Gospels all establish that Jesus of Nazareth is the Christ, the Messiah, the Anointed, by virtue of his special anointing with the Holy Spirit; and they all go on to present Jesus as both the *unique bearer of the Spirit* and the *unique baptiser with the Spirit*.

At the time of Jesus, there was a general feeling that the Holy Spirit had departed from Israel: God had not spoken through a prophet for several hundred years, and his glory no longer shone in the temple. So Jews looked back to the past with fond nostalgia and forward to the Messiah with expectant hope.

Mark's Gospel leaps over the nativity, cuts straight to the action, and presents Jesus' baptism as the great fulfilment of all these Old Testament hopes. In his first verse, Mark introduces Jesus as 'the Christ, the Son of God', and then immediately makes two radical claims.

Mark 1:11 ☐

Psalm 2:7 ☐

2 Samuel 7:14 ☐

Isaiah 42:1 ☐

First, he declares that God's silence has ended: for the first time since the age of Haggai, Zechariah and Malachi, God has spoken from heaven. As we have seen, the heavenly words recorded in Mark 1:11 combine the messianic hope of Psalm 2:7 and 2 Samuel 7:14 with the promise of a suffering Servant in Isaiah 42:1, and reveal Jesus as the unique being who is both Messianic Ruler and Suffering Servant.

Mark 1:15 ☐

Second, Mark declares that the drought of the Spirit is finally over. God has poured out his Holy Spirit to equip the Messianic Servant for his unique mission. It is no wonder that, according to Mark 1:15, Jesus' first words are, 'The time is fulfilled'.

THE SON UNIQUELY BEARS THE SPIRIT

Mark 13:11 ☐

Throughout his Gospel, Mark takes pains to show that the Son bears the Spirit during his time of earthly ministry and that the Son uniquely bears the Spirit during his days on the earth. Only in Mark 13:11, when Jesus is preparing his disciples for the end times, does Mark reveal that the Spirit will equip and enable anyone other than the Son.

Matthew 1:18–20 ☐

It is much the same in Matthew's Gospel, which also stresses that Jesus is the unique bearer of the Spirit. Matthew, however, imparts the extra information that Jesus was conceived by the Spirit: Matthew 1:18–20 shows that the Son was uniquely associated with the Spirit from the very outset of his life on earth.

Luke reveals more about the Spirit than the other Gospels, and emphasises the presence and activity of the Spirit in the nativity stories.

Although Luke shows that Mary, Elisabeth and Zechariah were also filled with the Spirit and empowered to prophesy, he lays tremendous stress on the Spirit activating the whole life and ministry of the Son.

He shows, for example, that the Holy Spirit led the Son into the wilderness, that the Son was filled with the power of the Spirit when he began his ministry, and that the Isaiah 61:1 anointing with the Spirit dominated and directed his whole ministry.

John 3:34 ☐

John's Gospel adds one further revelation about the way that the Son uniquely bears the Spirit. In John 3:34, when Jesus was speaking with John the Baptist's disciples, he claimed that God had given him the Holy Spirit 'without measure', without any reserve. In this remarkable way, we see that the Son truly stands alone in history as the only person who has ever received an *unlimited* anointing with the Spirit.

THE SON UNIQUELY BAPTISES WITH THE SPIRIT

All four Gospels agree that the Son not only uniquely bears the Spirit, but that he also uniquely baptises with the Spirit. This means that nobody can receive the Spirit except through the Son, and that nobody can know the Son except through the Spirit.

All four Gospels (and Acts) record John the Baptist's promise that Jesus will baptise with the Spirit – Matthew 3:1–12; Mark 1:1–8; Luke 3:1–18; John 1:19–34 and Acts 1:1–5. In fact, we can say that, wherever a study of Jesus begins, it is impossible to avoid the conclusion that – as far as John the Baptist is concerned – the most important task the Son would perform would be to baptise people in the Holy Spirit.

Matthew 3:1–12 ☐

Mark 1:1–8 ☐

Luke 3:1–18 ☐

John 1:19–34 ☐

Acts 1:1–5 ☐

When we come to the Gospels with fresh eyes, it can seem surprising that – after this introduction to the Son's Spirit-baptising mission – they then describe the Son doing everything except baptising with the Spirit.

But the whole New Testament teaches that the Son can give the Spirit only after he has been glorified in his death, resurrection and ascension. Every Gospel looks forward to the day when the Son will send the Spirit and equip the disciples to share in his mission. We see this, for example, in Matthew 28:19; Mark 13:11; Luke 11:13; 24:44–49; John 7:39 and 20:21–23; and we consider this fully in *Knowing the Spirit*.

Matthew 28:19 ☐

Mark 13:11 ☐

Luke 11:13 ☐
24:44–49 ☐

John 7:39 ☐
20:21–23 ☐

In summary, we can say the Gospels show that:

* *the Son was equipped for his unique mission by the Spirit*

* *the Spirit was not available to others during the Son's earthly life*

* *after the Son's death, resurrection and ascension, the Son gave the Spirit to his followers to equip them to continue his mission.*

THE SON REVEALS THE SPIRIT

We have noted that the revelation of God to humanity was an important aspect of the Son's multi-faceted mission. This means that the Son reveals the Spirit just as he reveals the Father.

We consider the work of Spirit in the Old Testament in *Knowing the Spirit*, and see that he was the very power of God – the unpredictable, hurricane of God's breath-wind. In the New Testament, however, the Spirit is no longer encountered as naked power; instead, he is clothed in the person and character of the Son. As Acts 16:7 and Philippians 1:19 explain (in most versions of the Bible), he is 'the Spirit of Jesus'.

This means that not only does the Son depend on the Spirit for power, direction and enabling, but that the Spirit also depends on the Son for revelation. We see this same divine mutual interdependence in the relationship between the Son and the Father in Part Seven.

John's Gospel strongly emphasises both the Son/Spirit and the Father/Son interdependence – the Son/Spirit relationship is particularly clear in, for example, John 16:7. We can say that, when the Son was on earth, he localised the presence of the Spirit; and that, now the Son is in heaven, the Spirit universalises the presence of the Son.

The Son was always limited by space and time in his earthly life, but his ascension made possible the coming of the Spirit who is not limited by any space/time barriers. Now, in the Spirit, the Son can permanently be with *all* his people – we can all be in him and he can be in all us.

The *Parakletos*

In John's Gospel, the Son reveals the Spirit as the *Parakletos*. This literally means 'called alongside' and can be translated as Advocate, Counsellor, Comforter, Helper, Intercessor, Support or Guide. We see this in John 14:15–18, 25–27; 15:26–27; 16:7–15.

John 14:16 uses the Greek word *allos* for 'another', instead of the alternative word *heteros*. This conclusively establishes that the *Parakletos* is 'another of the same type' not 'another of a different type' to Jesus. As we gaze at the Son, so we gain an insight into the Spirit; as we listen to the Spirit, so we hear the voice of the Son.

Acts 16:7 □

Philippians 1:19 □

John 14:15–18 □
14:25–27 □
15:26–27 □
16:7–15 □

John 14:18 underlines this even more strongly: in this verse, Jesus promises that he will *himself* come to his disciples in-and-through the sending of the Holy Spirit.

In the Old Testament, it seems that God allowed Moses and Elijah (who were especially anointed with the Spirit) to pass on their anointing to their chosen successors: we see this in Deuteronomy 34:9 and 2 Kings 2:9–15. Joshua and Elisha then continued Moses' and Elijah's ministries, with a similar anointing.

Deuteronomy 34:9 ☐

2 Kings 2:9–15 ☐

In the same way, Jesus (who was anointed with the Spirit without limit) was also allowed to pass on the Spirit to his chosen successors so that they could continue his mission. This means that the link between the Spirit and the Son has very important consequences for the way that we live and serve as disciples today.

This link between the Spirit and the Son means that the Spirit now acts in the same way as the Son acted in his earthly mission.

- *the Son came from the Father as the Father's gift to humanity, so does the Parakletos* – John 3:16; 5:43; 16:28

John 3:16 ☐
5:43 ☐
16:28 ☐
14:26 ☐
14:16–18 ☐

- *the Father sent the Son into the world as his representative, so the Son sends the Spirit in his name* – John 5:43; 14:26

- *the Son remained with and guided the disciples, so the Spirit will remain with and guide the disciples* – John 14:16–18

- *the Son taught his disciples the truth because he was the truth in person, so the Spirit of truth will lead the disciples into all the truth about Jesus* – John 14:6, 17; 15:26; 16:13

John 14:6 ☐
14:17 ☐
15:26 ☐
16:13 ☐

- *the Son did not draw attention to himself but glorified the Father by passing on the Father's message to humanity, so the Parakletos will not speak on his own authority but will only take what is the Son's and pass it on to the world* – John 8:28; 12:28; 16:14; 17:4

- *the Son bore witness to the Father, so the Spirit will bear witness to Jesus* – John 8:14; 15:26–27

John 8:28 ☐
12:28 ☐
16:14 ☐
17:4 ☐
8:14 ☐
15:26–27 ☐

The *Parakletos* does not only universalise the Son's presence to disciples, he also does the same to unbelievers in the world. Just as Jesus came to reach the lost and hurting, so John 15:26–27 teaches that the Spirit comes to witness to the world and to enable disciples to witness to the world.

John 16:8–11 ☐

John 16:8–11 goes on to explain that the Spirit will convict people that they are wrong about sin, righteousness and judgement. This, however, will not be a new revelation, for it is exactly what the Son has been doing throughout his earthly ministry – we see this in, for example, John 9:35–41. In fact, we can say that:

John 9:35–41 ☐

- *just as the world refused to accept the Son, so it will refuse to accept the Spirit – John 1:10–11; 14:17*

John 1:10–11 ☐
14:17 ☐

- *just as the Son bore witness against a background of hatred and opposition because he told people the unwelcome truth, so will the Spirit – John 7:7; 16:8*

John 7:7 ☐
16:8 ☐

THE SPIRIT OF SONSHIP

Every aspect of the Son's' ministry was shot through by the Spirit – he was the source of Jesus' life, his power and his emotions. For example:

Luke 10:21 ☐

- *he was filled with joy by the Spirit – Luke 10:21*

Matthew 12:28 ☐

- *he cast out demons by the Spirit – Matthew 12:28*

Acts 1:2 ☐

- *he taught by the Spirit – Acts 1:2*

Hebrews 9:14 ☐

- *he sacrificed himself by the Spirit – Hebrews 9:14*

Acts 10:38 ☐

- *he did good and cured all who had fallen into the power of the devil – Acts 10:38*

All this should be obvious, and we study the way that the Son ministers in-and-through the Spirit in *Knowing the Spirit*, *Ministry in the Spirit* and *Listening to God*.

The Spirit, however, also affected the Son at the fundamental level of his very sonship. We see in *Knowing the Father* that Jesus' sonship differs from ours. For example, he was born by the express agency of the Holy Spirit, but we are not; and he was Son of God by right, whereas we are sons of God only by adoption.

Nevertheless, it was possession of the Spirit which set Jesus apart as messianic Son of God and brought forth the voice from heaven at his baptism that declared his beloved sonship.

It was only as beloved Son that Jesus could call God 'Abba'. It was only the One who was set apart by the Spirit as the favoured Son of God who could dare to address God in this way – for only the Anointed enjoys the intimate relation of sonship with God the Father.

Of course, it is precisely this sonship which the Son creates for us. It is through the Spirit that the Son enables us to know the Father as 'Abba'. And it is through the Son that the Spirit adopts us alongside Christ into this sonship with God, and enables us to cry 'Abba' in the family of God. We see this in Romans 8:14–17 and consider it fully in *Knowing the Father*.

Romans 8:14–17 ☐

This is our incredible privilege and status as believers. We possess the Spirit of God's Son, and this makes us sons of God and enables us to utter the family cry. Truly it has been said that the whole of the good news can be concentrated into the single word 'Abba' – and this is the work of the Spirit of sonship.

THE SPIRIT OF SERVANTHOOD

In *Knowing the Father*, we note how Mark 14:35–36 reveals Jesus addressing God as 'Abba' when he is waiting for Judas in the Garden of Gethsemane in the shadow of the cross. We also consider the redemptive, trinitarian background of Isaiah 63:7–16 and Psalm 89:19–26, and see that approaching the Father as 'Abba' therefore involves accepting the suffering and sacrifice of the cross.

Mark 14:35–36 ☐

Isaiah 63:7–16 ☐

Psalm 89:19–26 ☐

Unlike the Old Testament kings who had aspired to the title 'Son of *Yahweh*', the Son displayed total trust in his Father even when it meant facing betrayal and the cross, and even when it involved great sacrifice and suffering. For the Son, sonship could not be separated from servanthood – for he had been anointed with the Spirit at his baptism to be the suffering Servant *as well as* the kingly Messiah.

When the Spirit came upon Jesus at his baptism, Mark 1:10 shows that he came 'like a dove'. This is most significant, for Leviticus 5:7–10 reports that the dove is an acceptable sin offering for a poor man and the only bird allowed as a sacrifice. Mary and Joseph brought two doves to the temple when they consecrated Jesus to the Lord.

Mark 1:10 ☐

Leviticus 5:7–10 ☐

At the Jordan, another dove appeared as Jesus was consecrated a second time, this time for service. The Hebrew word for dove is *Yonah*: Jonah, Mr Dove, was sent to a far pagan country on a mission to proclaim repentance, to save sinners, and he had to spend three days in the belly of a great fish before his 'resurrection'.

So, when the Spirit came down like a dove on the Son, he was revealing the Son's calling to be the suffering Servant who was called to preach repentance, to save sinners, to die and rise again after three days. The Son was to be the obedient Jonah. His serving mission would be even more successful than Jonah's. Ninevah would be saved, and all because the Spirit of servanthood had come upon the Son.

Once again, this has real consequences for our anointed lives of service. When the Son baptises us with the Spirit, he is calling us to trust God in the darkness and agony of our own Gethsemane, and to obey when our inclination is to go an easier way. This is a consistent theme of the New Testament, for example:

Acts 4:29–31 ☐
- *Acts 4:29–31 records it is when the first believers suffer for Christ that they return to their friends, pray for boldness (not safety) and are shaken by the Spirit.*

Acts 20:22–23 ☐
- *Acts 20:22–23 shows that it is the Spirit who convinces Paul that imprisonment and afflictions await him in Jerusalem and constrain him to accept this destiny.*

1 Peter 4:13–16 ☐
- *1 Peter 4:13–16 stresses that the Spirit calls us into the experience of Christ's sufferings.*

THE SPIRIT OF WITNESS

The dove at Jesus' baptism did not only point to Jonah's suffering service, it also pointed to Jonah's effective witness. A dove first appeared in the Bible in Genesis 8:1–12, and then it was as a witness both to God's new creation and to Noah's family's new life in the abundant promises of God.

Genesis 8:1–12 ☐

The dove-like Spirit of witness came upon the Son at the Jordan, and immediately the Son began witnessing in the power of the Spirit.

We see this in Luke 4:18, and it was the same for the disciples after their anointing with the Spirit by the Son at Pentecost.

The book of Acts opens with a nervous group of about 120 disciples huddling to pray in a private room; yet it goes on to describe how they became a body of powerful witnesses who overcame fierce opposition to establish a flourishing church throughout the Roman Empire.

The Spirit of witness can be seen on every page of Acts, as people are healed, delivered, converted, empowered and transformed into credible witnesses of the risen Son. And the Holy Spirit is always the main reason for the disciples' effectiveness.

In *Knowing the Spirit*, we see that witness is the essence of the Holy Spirit. John 15:26–27 shows that the Spirit's two greatest purposes are:

- *to testify about the Son*

- *to help us to bear witness to the Son*

And Acts 1:8 promises that the Spirit's anointing always results in:

- *disciples becoming powerful witnesses to the Son*

In *Knowing the Spirit*, we establish that the Spirit always brings decisive change. He wants to fill us with the Son's power and purity, to direct us to perform the Son's work, and to enable us to live in the Son's presence: and he wants to do all this so that we *know the Son* better and make him better known.

All these great works of the Spirit, however, relate to his primary purpose of witness. We have noted, in Luke 4:18, that Jesus claimed he had been anointed with the Spirit especially to evangelise the hurting. And we see the same purpose behind anointing throughout the rest of the New Testament – whenever people are filled or anointed with the Holy Spirit, effective witness soon starts to take place.

Passages like Acts 2:41–47; 4:31–33; 6:10; 9:17–28; 10:44–46; 13:9–12; 19:6–20; 1 Thessalonians 1:5–8; Hebrews 2:4; 1 Peter 1:12 show that magnifying God and witnessing to Jesus were the direct consequence of people receiving the Spirit of witness from the Son.

We can say that the urge to witness was bred into the church by the Spirit. At Pentecost, the church became a naturally 'witnessing-to-the-Son' church because the Spirit of witness had come upon it. We see this in passages like Acts 4:20.

Luke 4:18 ☐

John 15:26–27 ☐

Acts 1:8 ☐

Acts 2:41–47 ☐
4:31–33 ☐
6:10 ☐
9:17–28 ☐
10:44–46 ☐
13:9–12 ☐
19:6–20 ☐

1 Thessalonians
1:5–8 ☐

Hebrews 2:4 ☐

1 Peter 1:12 ☐

Acts 4:20 ☐

When we have drawn together the threads of sonship, servanthood and witness, and have recognised that the Spirit is the Spirit of Jesus, we should begin expect to see similar marks of the Spirit in the lives of the Son's anointed followers.

The New Testament shows, for example, that the Spirit enables the Son's disciples:

- *to be a witness to Jesus* – Acts 1:8
- *to witness to Jesus' resurrection* – Acts 4:33
- *to do great wonders and signs* – Acts 6:8
- *to do good and heal* – Acts 10:38
- *to abound in hope* – Romans 15:13
- *to perform mighty signs and wonders* – Romans 15:18–19
- *to speak and preach* – 1 Corinthians 2:4–5
- *to endure difficulties* – 2 Corinthians 6:6–10
- *to rejoice in weakness* – 2 Corinthians 12:9
- *to be strengthened to know God's love* – Ephesians 3:16
- *to stand against the enemy in prayer* – Ephesians 6:10–18
- *to announce the gospel* – 1 Thessalonians 1:5
- *to be patient* – Colossians 1:11
- *to share in Christ's sufferings* – 2 Timothy 1:8

This means that we should surely expect 'the Spirit of Jesus' to work in a similar way in our lives today. We should expect the Spirit to bring us a deep assurance that we really are adopted sons of God. We should expect him to call us along the pathway of service, and to be ready to share the Son's suffering with joy. And we should expect the Spirit to send us out and to witness to the Son with his personal power and effectiveness.

PART SEVEN

the son and the father

In *Knowing the Father*, we begin by considering the trinitarian relationships between the Father, the Son and the Spirit, and then we focus on the Father's relationship with the Son. We see that:

- *the Father depends on the Son, and has committed everything to him; the Father does not act, or speak, or give himself apart from the Son*

- *the Father exercises his sovereignty in communion with the Son, who enacts and reveals the Father's will*

- *the Father expresses his identity in the Son, because it is the Son who makes him known*

- *the Father is identical with the Son in being and nature*

- *the Father works in partnership with the Son in creation, redemption and judgement*

- *the Father's relationship with the Son is at the heart of the gospel, for fatherhood and sonship imply both mutual dependence and shared life*

Although the Father's depends on the Son for his identity, his revelation and his actions, this is not the full story of the Godhead. We also need to understand that the Son depends fully on the Father and always submits completely to him.

THE SON RECEIVES HIS IDENTITY FROM THE FATHER

Just as we see in *Knowing the Father* that the Father is identified in his relationship with the Son, so the Son receives his identity in his relationship with the Father. And he does not receive it only once, but time and again at every stage of his unique mission.

At each crisis in the Son's living and dying, he received a fresh confirmation of his personal identity: he came to know again his relationship with the Father through yet another confession of 'Abba' in the power of the Spirit.

Defining identity

Throughout the ages, men and women have looked in many different directions to discover who they really are. Some people look *inwards* to define themselves psychologically; others look *backwards* to define themselves in terms of the past from which they have sprung; and still more look *outwards* to define themselves in terms of their achievements.

Jesus related to all these ways of identifying and defining himself. He knew the Father in deep inward experience; but he did not trust in this experience itself. Instead, he trusted only in the reality and authority of the Father who spoke to him within the inner experience.

He knew that his historical roots were the best and the deepest, for he was descended from king David and was part of Israel's royal line of promise. Yet Jesus was not bound by his past and family traditions, for his ultimate dependence was always upon his heavenly Father rather than his earthly line.

And he had a long catalogue of great achievements to prove his messianic claim – we see these, for example, in Matthew 11:4–6. But these were the fruit, rather than the source, of his confidence in who he was. Jesus' works flowed from his sonship, they did not make him the Son. He cast out demons, healed and proclaimed the kingdom *because* he was the Anointed Son. His ministry was his obedience to his identity rather than his way of achieving his identity. His relationship with the Father always came before his service with-and-for the Father.

Matthew 11:4–6 □

We can say, therefore, that Jesus was given his identity as Son through his experience, his tradition and his mission. He knew that he was 'the Christ, the Son of the living God' not merely by knowing that he was, but because he knew the Father: Quite simply, Jesus knew himself as Son because he knew God as Father.

Jesus in the temple

Luke 2:41–50 relates how Jesus stayed behind in the temple when his parents left Jerusalem. Much of the story's significance lies in the fact that it happened in the year Jesus attained Jewish adulthood.

Luke 2:41–50 □

It was his youthful realisation that God was his Father which made him relegate his relationship with his parents to second place. He suddenly grasped that the Father had first claim on his attention, his loyalty and his obedience: the Son must be about the Father's business.

In Luke 2:49, Jesus' first recorded words (like his last on the cross in 23:46) describe his relationship with the Father. This could be Luke's way of saying that, with the Son, his relationship with the Father comes first and last and everywhere in-between.

Luke 23:46 □

Jesus at the Jordan

We have seen that Jesus' realisation of his sonship is a vital part of his baptism. As the Son rises from the water and consecrates himself to his mission, the Father speaks and the Spirit comes down. As the apostle Paul teaches in Romans 8:15–17, a new awareness of sonship and a new release of the Spirit are closely connected.

Romans 8:15–17 □

When Jesus realises afresh that he is the Son, he enters into the Son's inheritance. He leaves the Jordan with a new confidence of sonship, and begins to exercise the Spirit's authority which is his right as Son.

We have noted that the Father's words echo Psalm 2:7–8 and Isaiah 42:1, and identify Jesus as Messiah and Servant. We should recognise that they also echo Genesis 22:2–16, where Isaac is identified as 'your only and beloved son'. This is a clear prophetic pointer to a sacrificial son: what Abraham was at the last moment excused from giving, the Father was now making ready to give – his only and beloved Son.

Jesus in the wilderness

Luke's account of the Son's temptations, in 4:1–13, focuses on the devil's attack on the fresh consciousness of sonship which came to Jesus at his baptism. The first and third temptations both begin with 'If you are the Son . . .' and challenge the validity and authority of the voice which spoke at the Jordan.

The first temptation attacks the Son's obedience: he is tempted to use his own power to meet his needs for bread rather than to obey the Father's words to him. The third temptation attacks the Son's trust in what his Father has said to him: he is tempted to prove his sonship because he no longer believes it. The devil suggests that an experimental leap will provide the proof which the Son needs. Satan insists that it is not enough for the Son to hear the Father speak, he should also use his power to demonstrate to himself that he really is the Son. Wonderfully, Jesus exposes and defeats both temptations.

The appropriate relationship of a son to a father is dependence, which consists of obedient trust and trusting obedience, and it is significant that Jesus is attacked by Satan at both these points. If the Son fails here, his whole mission will fail before it has begun.

With the temptations over and his trust and obedience affirmed, Jesus moves to Nazareth sure that he is the obedient Son who has believed what his Father has spoken. He is the Son on whom the favour and Spirit of the Father rests; he can go forward against all opposition knowing that the Father is with him and will honour what he has said.

Jesus at his transfiguration

At the hour of his critical decision to turn towards Calvary, Jesus is once again told who he is by the Father. He has taught the disciples that he is going to Jerusalem to suffer and die, and the transfiguration is God's confirmation of this choice. First, Moses and Elijah, the law and the prophets, speak to him. Then the Father speaks, repeating the words spoken at the Jordan – but with two significant differences.

In Luke 9:35, the word *eklelegmenos*, 'chosen' replaces *agapetos*, 'beloved'; and the phrase *autou akouete*, 'hear him', replaces 'with whom I am well pleased. Because Jesus has been chosen to walk the path of obedient suffering (and has chosen to walk it), he has a new right to be heard, a new authority among men and women.

Luke 9:35 ☐

As the Son prepares to glorify the Father in his death, so the Father prepares to glorify the Son with a new identification and authentication of his mission. Quite simply, sonship means being chosen for costly obedience *and* being brought into a position of authority.

Jesus in the garden

As Jesus begins his agony in the garden of Gethsemane, so he finds his strength in reaffirming his relationship with 'Abba'. He is able to take the cup of God's wrath, rejection and judgement because the hand that offers the cup is still the hand of his Father.

Luke 22:43 shows that there was not only prayer and pleading by the Son in Gethsemane, but also revelation and strengthening from the Father. It is only in the strength of this communion with the Father that the Son can face his passion.

Luke 22:43 ☐

Jesus on the cross

Luke emphasises this again by reporting that two of Jesus' sentences on the cross are 'Abba' sentences – Luke 23:34 and 23:46.

Luke 23:34 ☐
23:46 ☐

The first of these shows that forgiveness of others is mediated through the Son's prayer to the Father on the cross. The second (which echoes Jesus' youthful words in the temple) shows that the Son dies in peace and confidence because he knows that God is still his Father.

In the garden, 'Abba' was the one who had to be obeyed when he made his unconditional demands. On the cross, 'Abba' is the one whom can be trusted for ultimate comfort: the Son's active obedience which has given everything in sacrifice becomes passive trust which accepts everything in death.

We can say that, from the teenager in the temple to the man on the cross, at every critical point of temptation, decision, suffering and death, Jesus always finds his identity and confidence as Son in his relationship with his Father.

At every point of need, God provides him with a fresh revelation of fatherhood and sonship, and it is this which strengthens Jesus to respond to the Father with trust and obedience.

THE SON DEPENDS ON THE FATHER

We establish in *Knowing the Father* that the Father depends on the Son; now we need to grasp that the Son depends on the Father.

The Son depends on the Father because it is the Father who reveals the Son and makes him known – just as it is the Son who reveals the Father and makes him known to others. This is another example of the divine mutual interdependence that we considered in Part Six.

The Son glorifies the Father (makes him known in his presence, his nature and his power) and the Father bears witness to the Son and glorifies the Son. This means that there is a reciprocal glorification of Father and Son in the words and works of Jesus.

It is worth noting that the Gospels of Matthew and John tend to attribute to the Father the work of bringing people into a recognition and confession of the mystery and person of Jesus; whereas the rest of the New Testament tends to attribute this work to the Holy Spirit.

This demonstrates that there is a basic unity between the work of the Father and the work of the Spirit. After all, the Spirit is the Father and the Son reaching out in communication and love beyond themselves towards one another; the work of revelation, therefore, can rightly be attributed to each of them singly and to all of them jointly.

Matthew 11:27 □

We consider Matthew 11:27 in some detail in *Knowing the Father*, and see that exclusive knowledge of the Father is attributed to the Son, and that exclusive knowledge of the Son is attributed to the Father. They depend on each other, and this is the fundamental relationship which undergirds both revelation and salvation: we are able to know each of them only through the activity of the other one.

We can see this in Matthew 16:17, where Jesus states that Peter's confession of Jesus as Messiah and Son of God is the work of the Father and not that of Peter. (Interestingly, 1 Corinthians 12:3 ascribes an almost identical confession to the work of the Holy Spirit. This is not a contradiction, for it is now the Spirit who executes the Father's will on earth in revealing his truth, love, grace and power to humanity.)

Matthew 16:17 ☐

1 Corinthians 12:3 ☐

John 6

In John 6:22–66, Jesus repeatedly acknowledges his dependence on the Father's activity when people 'come to him'.

John 6:22–66 ☐

In verse 36, he contrasts 'seeing' and 'believing' by saying that some people have seen him but not believed. Throughout this passage, Jesus explains what it is that decides whether those who 'see' the Son will also 'believe' in him (verse 40), be 'drawn' to him (verse 44), 'come' to him (verse 65), and so on. He insists that it is *the Father* who gives him disciples (verse 37), who draws people (verse 44), and enables them to come to him (verse 65).

Whenever somebody comes to Jesus – behind the human confession, following and discipleship – there is a Fatherly choosing, revealing and enabling which Jesus recognises and proclaims.

Of course, the Father's gracious action does not exclude the necessity or the genuineness of the human action; rather, it precedes, enables and sustains the human action. We can say that the Father's choice is behind the human choosing; that the Father's drawing is behind the human coming; that the Father's revealing is behind the human believing, and so on.

Verse 37 shows that Jesus is bound to receive all those who come to him, because he knows that their coming does not have its origin in either him or them, but in the Father. This means that the obedient Son receives all whom the sovereign Father sends.

John's Gospel describes the Spirit doing much the same thing as the Father: we see this, for example, in John 3:5; 6:63 and 16:15. Most scholars interpret this as basic biblical trinitarianism; some, however, suggest that there is a difference between the Father's sovereign revelation to a person and the Spirit's gracious enabling of that person's decision; while a few scholars argue that the Father works

John 3:5 ☐
6:63 ☐
16:15 ☐

outwardly creating providentially constructive circumstances and that the Spirit works inwardly creating inner spiritual openness.

Whatever the precise relationship between the work of the Father and the Spirit, it is plain that the Son depends on the Father to reveal him to people and bring them to him. We can say that Jesus depends completely on the Father to glorify his Son and make him known.

THE SON SUBMITS TO THE FATHER

We see in *Knowing the Father* that the Father's will is executed through the Son as its essential agent; now we need to grasp that every action of the Son depends upon, and is determined by, the Father.

Every word and deed of Jesus originates from, is guided by, and is directed towards the person, purpose and glory of the Father. He is fully submitted to the Father, not to an impersonal rule or regulation.

From first to last, the Son's words and deeds are always obedient actions. He never presumes or disobeys, and he never initiates or innovates; instead, he always discerns and follows the Father's will. This does not limit his spontaneity and freedom; rather, it is its source – because the Son responds to everything and everyone within the context of his relationship with the Father.

The Father is the source of the Son's mission

The whole New Testament underlines that Jesus is the *apostolos*, 'the one sent' by the Father with a mission to fulfil which the Father has given him. For example, Hebrews 10:7 quotes Psalm 40:8 and identifies the Son's essential motivation and energising purpose.

Hebrews 10:7 ☐

Psalm 40:8 ☐

John 6:38 ☐

John's Gospel relentlessly stresses this. John 6:38 stands for a host of verses which all say the same thing – that the Son came from heaven not to do his will but to do the will of the one who sent him.

John 20:21 ☐

At the very end of the Gospel, in John 20:21, Jesus calls and integrates his disciples into the very same mission to which his Father has called and sent him.

The Father controls the Son's mission

In Luke 7:8, a Roman centurion instinctively recognises that Jesus is a man under authority – and it is always the authority of his Father.

Luke 7:8 ☐

Within Jesus' earthly life, there was a secret, commanding, continuous, personal guidance which shaped his every decision. As a result, the Son's will, words, thoughts and actions were continually submitted to the Father's will, words, thoughts and actions.

Once again, this is especially clear in John's Gospel: John 5:19–20 is typical, and shows that the Son *never* does anything of his own; instead, he always does *only* what he sees the Father doing. This is not a dry theological principle; it is a living description of the Son's daily submitted life.

John 5:19–20 ☐

The Father is the future of the Son's mission

We can say that the Father is the future of the Son's mission in the double sense that the completed work of the Son is submitted to the Father's verdict, *and* that he builds the kingdom for the Father and – when it is completed – will hand it to the Father. We see this in 1 Corinthians 15:28.

1 Corinthians 15:28 ☐

The apostle Paul's description of the Son's submission and subordination to the Father, in 1 Corinthians 15, seems to represent the apostle's understanding of the Father's absolute priority.

In this chapter, Paul explains that everything came from the Father through Christ at the beginning, and that everything will all return to the Father through Christ at the end. It is all from-and-for the Father, through the Son.

Paul states this idea rather more simply in Philippians 2:10. He shows there that the coming widespread confession of Jesus' lordship will not be for the Son's glory but will be to glorify the Father.

Philippians 2:10 ☐

This suggests that the Son's unique mission is:

- *from the Father as its initiating source*

- *with the Father as its continuing authority*

- *for the Father as its ultimate purpose*

THE SON LISTENS TO THE FATHER

The Son's active submission to the Father, which – as we stress throughout this *Sword of the Spirit* series – is the essence of his sonship (and, therefore, of our sonship) presupposes the Son's active, continuous listening to the Father.

The Son's earthly communication with the heavenly Father expresses in human form the unique eternal communication of Father and Son in the Spirit. The way in which the Father guides the incarnate Son is exactly the same way that he guides us, even though the purpose of the Son's guidance is different from ours. We consider this more fully in *Listening to God*.

The Son listens through events

The Father shows the Son what he is doing in the world, not mainly by spiritual visions, but largely in the context of the human events which are going on in the world around him.

The Gospels show that Jesus was wide open to his world and to all the activities of the men and women around him: this is the arena within which the Father shows the Son what he is doing.

This, surely, is the main reason why Jesus teaches so extensively through parables. In one sense, the stories of the Woman and her coin, the Servant and his debt, the Farmer and his crops, do not amount to a special spiritual revelation. But in another sense – to the one who has eyes to see and ears to hear – they are the language in which the Father speaks to his Son and, through him, to all his children.

When we recognise that Jesus speaks only what he hears the Father say, we are forced to conclude that it is the Father himself who speaks in simple, 'worldly' parables. This realisation should transform the way that we preach and proclaim the gospel.

We can say that, in part, Jesus came to see that his was the way of the cross through the reactions of ordinary people – and especially the religious authorities – to him. As the Son discerned the needs and responses that met him in the villages of Galilee, so his Father showed him what awaited him in Jerusalem, and why it was only through death and resurrection that his purpose could be fulfilled.

This suggests that, if we do not know the world in which we have been placed by the Father, we will not know what the Father wants to do through us in the world.

The Son listens to the Old Testament

The Father also spoke to the Son through the past traditions of the Jewish people, for these had been the place of his action and self-revelation for almost two thousand years. What the Father willed to do through the Son merely continued and fulfilled what he had long been doing in Israel, and what was clearly recorded in the Old Testament.

Jesus' communication with Moses and Elijah, at his transfiguration, was merely an intensification of his communication with 'the law and the prophets' in which the Son had listened to the Father throughout his earthly life.

All his teaching shows that the Son was steeped in the Old Testament, but he handled it with amazing boldness and freedom – 'not like the scribes'. Through listening to the Father in-and-through the Scriptures, Jesus grasped that his personal fulfilment of the biblical promises would be startlingly different from what was imagined by the people of his day.

The Gospels show that the Son was almost bound to the Old Testament. Every time that the Father spoke to him, it was in words which echo the Old Testament. When Jesus resisted Satan's temptations in the wilderness; when he announced his mission statement in Nazareth; when he instituted his memorial meal in the upper room; even when he spoke on the cross – it was all a fresh application of the ageless Old Testament.

The Son's knowledge of, dependence on, and careful listening to the Father in the Old Testament is one of the primary reasons for the *Sword of the Spirit's* considerable emphasis on the complete canon of Scripture.

When the people around Jesus (and we today) sought to understand the Son and his work, they had to use categories and phrases like 'Son of Man', 'kingdom', 'Messiah', 'Son of David', 'servant of God', and so on, which can be understood correctly only when they are interpreted both by their Old Testament origin *and* by the new meaning which Jesus gave them through his life and death.

Mark 1:35 ☐

Luke 6:12 ☐

Luke 3:21 ☐

Mark 1:35 ☐
        6:46 ☐

Luke 5:16 ☐

Luke 6:12 ☐
        9:18 ☐
        9:28–29 ☐

John 17 ☐

Mark 14:32 ☐

Luke 22:41 ☐
        22:32 ☐

Matthew
        19:13–15 ☐

Luke 23:34 ☐
        24:50 ☐

John 14:16 ☐

Matthew
        26:36–46 ☐

Mark 14:32–42 ☐

Luke 22:39–46 ☐

The Son listens in prayer

In *Effective Prayer*, we see just how much the Son was a man of prayer. This was the means by which the Son on earth communicated with the Father in heaven, and the Father communicated with the Son.

The Gospels (especially Luke) often describe the Son praying to the Father. For example, he prayed:

- *early in the morning* – Mark 1:35

- *late in the evening* – Luke 6:12

- *at his baptism* – Luke 3:21

- *after much ministry* – Mark 1:35, 6:46, Luke 5:16

- *for a night before selecting the twelve disciples* – Luke 6:12

- *alone in the presence of his disciples* – Luke 9:18

- *at his transfiguration* – Luke 9:28–29

- *after the last supper* – John 17

- *in Gethsemane* – Mark 14:32, Luke 22:41

- *for Peter* – Luke 22:32

- *for small children* – Matthew 19:13–15

- *at his crucifixion* – Luke 23:34

- *after his resurrection* – Luke 24:30

- *at his ascension* – Luke 24:50

- *after his ascension* – John 14:16

We consider Jesus' model prayer and his John 17 intercession in *Effective Prayer*; the Son's prayer at the foot of the Mount of Olives, however, suggests two important principles which seem to mark all the Son's prayerful communication with the Father.

Matthew 26:36–46; Mark 14:32–42 and Luke 22:39–46 show that Jesus' listening begins with confession – not of his sin, but of his situation and of his desires about it. The Son does not conceal what he wants from the Father; instead, he makes his desires clear. Even so, he submits his desire to the Father's will; he does not thrust his will on the Father with the pretext that *he* can ask for anything *he* likes.

Then, in his listening, he discerns his Father's will. As the Son prays in great agony, he grasps that what he began by asking cannot be given to him. He realises that what his Father is doing requires him to drink the cup dry. The Son only does what he sees the Father doing, and – in this listening prayer – he 'sees' the Father saving the world through his own sacrifice. Therefore, the Son aligns his will with the Father's.

The atmosphere changes as soon as the Son has 'heard' the Father's will. The agony is over and he rises peacefully to proceed to the cross.

At the central climax of his life, we see that the Son made time to listen to the Father in prayer and to discern what his Father was doing, where he was going, and what he was saying. Surely, however, the Son could do this in Gethsemane only because he had been listening in the same way, in less extreme situations, throughout his earthly life.

The Son obeys what he hears

Through living in the world, through the Old Testament, through listening prayer, the Son repeatedly grasped the Father's 'particular will' for specific situations. We consider this in *Living Faith*.

Throughout every aspect of his mission, in all his dealings with people, the Son acted situationally and creatively rather than by rule or principle. This is the action of the Spirit, by whom God gives his truth, love and power in ways which are uniquely relevant to each situation.

The Gospels show that, time and again, in the Holy Spirit, Jesus 'sees and hears' what his Father wants to do or say in that particular place, at that unique moment. As we see in *Ministry in the Spirit*, the Son never follows a method, never uses a technique, never follows spiritual principles; instead, he always listens to the Father, in the Spirit, and sees what the Father is doing then and there.

THE SON ACTS WITH THE FATHER

In the Gospels, the Son often claims that his words are the Father's words, and that his deeds are the Father's deeds – because his being is identical with the Father's: we see this in John 5:17 and 14:10–11.

John 5:17 ☐
14:10–11 ☐

This means that the Father speaks and acts through the words and deeds of the Son, that the Father loves and deals in salvation through the sacrifice of the Son, that the Father protects and provides for his children through the gifts and grace of the Son, and so on.

Through the Son, God reveals that he is the Father who makes the blind see, the deaf hear, the lame walk, the dead rise. He is the Father who works salvation – and whose words and works are known and effected through his Son. Quite simply, no word or work of the Son is not also a word and work of the Father.

It is a fundamental New Testament assumption that Jesus is the essential partner of the Father in all God's dealings with humanity. We must remember that the Son's words and actions are indispensable clues to the Father's purpose in creation, redemption and judgement.

They act together in creation

John 1:3 □

Colossians 1:15–17 □

Hebrews 1:2 □

John 1:3; Colossians 1:15–17 and Hebrews 1:2 show that the Father acts with-and-through the Son in creation.

The Son is the agent and the final purpose of all creation, and we should not think about God's work in creation without appreciating the Father/Son relationship which established and sustains it. In fact, we can say that the Father's actions with the Son surround everything to do with our natural universe.

They act together in redemption

John 3:16 □

2 Corinthians 5:18–19 □

It is the same in salvation, for our restored relationship with the Father depends entirely on the life, death and resurrection of the Son. Passages like John 3:16 and 2 Corinthians 5:18–19 shows how the Father's saving action moves from the one to many, from its centre in Christ to all humanity.

It is not enough for our understanding and celebration of redemption to focus only on the Son or only on the Father – we must appreciate that salvation depends on the Father acting in and through the Son.

The great purpose of redemption is that we might know the Father through the Son, and might live in fellowship with him in the sort of mutual dependence that we see between the Father and the Son.

They act together in judgement

It will be the same at the last day. The Father is the source of God's judgement, but it is the Son who executes his judgement – we see this throughout Revelation, and in John 3:18–21; 5:22 and Acts 17:31.

The Bile also shows that the Father and Son will act together at the last day in the completion of the kingdom and the establishment of the new heaven and earth. Ephesians 1:10; Philippians 2:9–11 and 1 Corinthians 15:28 reveal that the focus will be on the Son, but that the priority of the Father will be paramount.

John 3:18–21 ☐
5:22 ☐
Acts 17:31 ☐
Ephesians 1:10 ☐
Philippians
2:9–11 ☐
1 Corinthians
15:28 ☐

They act together in revelation

Every aspect of God's holy character can be seen and heard in the Father/Son relationship which was revealed 2,000 years ago on earth and is recorded now in the New Testament.

This means that we must move beyond thinking about God in abstract terms, and begin to appreciate what the Father and Son acting together really means. We can say, for example, that:

- *the love of God* is not a perfect ideal of love; it is the practical love which, in the person of the Son, comes to seek and to save those who are separated from the Father.

- *the power of God* is not vague omnipotence, it is the specific power by which the Son revealed the Father by becoming a human being, by healing the sick, by enduring the cross, by rising from the dead, and so on.

- *the truth of God* is not a body of ideas, it is the Father's thoughts which are expressed in the person, words and actions of the Son.

Thinking like this merely applies the truth of Matthew 11:27; it recognises that the Father has delivered all things to the Son, and that no one knows the Father except the Son – and those to whom the Son chooses to reveal him.

Matthew 11:27 ☐

We now turn to the most important joint-action of the Father and Son, to the final expression of the Son's full dependence on the Father and perfect submission to the Father. Just as the Father is the past from which the Son comes, and is the present in which the Son lives, so the cross is the future to which the Son goes with the Father.

PART EIGHT

the son and the cross

When we read the Gospels to learn about the Son's life, it is plain that his death on the cross is by far the most significant event. In fact, we can say that the shadow of the cross falls on every page of the Bible.

The cross must be the most important event in human history, and has become the universal symbol of our Christian faith. We consider it carefully throughout *Salvation by Grace*, and see just why the Father had to send the Son to die, and exactly what his death achieved.

We also examine the cross from the Father's particular point of view in *Knowing the Father*, and grasp that it was his gracious initiative, his sacrificial activity, his experience of grief.

In those two books in this *Sword of the Spirit* series, we take a biblical overview of the cross, consider the 'big picture' of salvation, and try to grasp its theological implications. The Gospels, however, present the cross in a rather different way. They lead us to the cross along the path walked by the Son – by way of the last supper, the agony in the garden, the betrayal by Judas, the arrest and trial, the torture and execution, the tomb and the glory, and so on.

The Gospels do not present the story of 'the Son and the cross' as an abstract theological theory, but as a personal drama which involves a company of players and is illuminated by many important details.

Most significantly, they record what the Son said and did in the hours of his greatest struggle – and these are what we consider in this chapter.

The Gospels set the drama of the Son's last twenty four hours on earth in four main locations:

- *the upper room*

- *the garden of Gethsemane*

- *the procurator's residence*

- *the place called Golgotha*

THE LAST SUPPER

The drama begins on the evening of the first day of the feast of Passover. Significantly, the Son was spending his last evening on earth by eating the Passover meal with his apostles in the large upper room of a friend's home.

It seems that no servant was present, for there was no-one to wash their feet before the meal began – and none of the apostles was humble enough to perform this menial task. So Jesus put on a servant's apron, poured water into a basin, and did what none of them had been willing to do. He then explained to the apostles that God's love always expresses itself in humble service, and that the world would recognise them as his disciples only if they loved each other in a similar way.

Next, he warned the apostles that one of them was going to betray him, revealed much about his impending departure, comforted them with news of the Spirit, and taught them about the Spirit's forth-coming work in the world and their lives.

Then, while the meal was still in progress, he gave thanks for a loaf of bread, broke it into pieces, and handed it around with the words recorded in Matthew 26:26–28; Mark 14:22–24 and Luke 22:17–19.

Matthew
        26:26–28 ☐

Mark 14:22–24 ☐

Luke 22:17–19 ☐

After the supper had ended, Jesus did the same with a cup of wine: he gave thanks for it, passed it around, and told the apostles what it symbolised. These are important words and actions which dramatise and explain Jesus' death before it occurs, and we consider them in *Glory in the Church*.

The Son's death is central

By his words in the upper room, the Son was giving instructions for his own memorial service – which he said should be held regularly. Jesus' words of institution show that, unlike modern memorial services, his should not commemorate his birth and life, nor his words and works, but only his atoning death.

Nothing underlines the significance that Jesus gives to his death more than these words at the last supper. It is plain that he wants us to remember him essentially by his death on the cross. If the cross is not central to our faith and to our worship, it is not the faith and worship that he is seeking.

The Son's death has purpose

Jesus' words of institution refer to a 'new covenant' and to 'forgiveness from sin', and we consider these phrases fully in *Salvation by Grace*.

God had entered into a covenant (a binding agreement) with Abram which promised him a land, great blessing, a personal relationship and a multitude of descendants. God renewed, and added to, this covenant after rescuing Abraham's descendants from Egypt. He promised to be their God and to make them his people, and he ratified this through the blood of a sacrifice which Moses sprinkled on the people.

About one thousand years later, the prophet Jeremiah promised that God would one day make a new covenant which would involve the forgiveness of sin and a radical change of heart – we see this in Jeremiah 31:31–34.

Jeremiah
31:31–34 ☐

At the last supper, after another six hundred years, the Son claimed that this promise was about to be fulfilled through the shedding of his blood in death. He said that he was going to the cross to die to bring his people into a new and unbreakable covenant relationship with God.

The Son's death must be personally appropriated

The apostles were not just spectators and listeners to the drama in the upper room, they were also active participants. The Son may have broken the bread, but the apostles had to eat it; the Son may have poured the cup, but the apostles had to receive it.

Just as it was not enough for the bread to be broken and the wine poured out, so it would not be enough for him to die – the apostles had to appropriate personally the benefits of his death. This was no more than Jesus had promised in John 6:53–55.

GETHSEMANE

John 18:2 ☐

Matthew
 26:36–46 ☐

Mark 14:32–42 ☐

Luke 22:39–46 ☐

After the supper, when Jesus had finished instructing the apostles and praying for them, they walked through Jerusalem to a garden called Gethsemane at the foot of the Mount of Olives. John 18:2 suggests that the Son had often visited this garden with his disciples.

Matthew 26:36–46; Mark 14:32–42 and Luke 22:39–46 report that the Son asked eight of his disciples to watch and pray while he went further with Peter, James and John. Jesus told them that he was overwhelmed with sorrow, 'to the point of death', and then asked them to keep watch for him. He then went deeper into the garden, fell prostrate to the ground, and prayed the climactic prayer of submission to the Father's will that we considered in Part Seven.

He returned to the apostles, found them asleep, remonstrated, and went away to wrestle again in prayer. Twice more he returned and found them sleeping, for they could not enter into the mystery of his suffering. Luke reports that Jesus' anguish was so great his sweat fell like drops of blood to the ground.

Job 21:20 ☐

Psalm 75:8 ☐

Isaiah 51:17–22 ☐

Jeremiah
 25:15–29 ☐
 49:12 ☐

Ezekiel 23:32–34 ☐

Habakkuk 2:16 ☐

Some people wonder how the Son of God could have been overwhelmed with grief and dread, how he could have begged to be spared the cup, how he could have flinched from God's will.

The Old Testament often describes God's wrath and judgement as 'a cup' – for example, Job 21:20; Psalm 75:8; Isaiah 51:17–22; Jeremiah 25:15–29; 49:12; Ezekiel 23:32–34 and Habakkuk 2:16.

The Son knew the Scriptures and must have recognised that the cup he was being offered contained the wine of God's wrath which was due only to the wicked.

Jesus knew that he was called to be so identified with sinners as to bear their judgement, and – in the garden – his sinless self recoiled from this. He may have hung back from experiencing the alienation from the Father which was inevitably involved with judgement, but he did not rebel or disobey the Father.

Jesus drew strength from the angels as he accepted the implications of his coming death. He knew that the cup would be given to him by the Father, and he was willing to drink it. So he waited quietly in the garden for Judas' kiss, and for his trials by the Jews and Romans to begin; he even spoke the words recorded in John 18:11.

John 18:11 ☐

THE TRIALS

The four Gospels present a complex drama which blends together a great host of factors in Jesus' death.

They record that the Son was publicly executed as a criminal because his teaching was considered to be dangerous and subversive. They show that the Jewish leaders were outraged by his seemingly disrespectful attitude to the law, while the Roman leaders were worried by his apparent challenge to Caesar's supreme authority.

Both groups of leaders were so disturbed by the Son that they forged an unholy alliance to do away with him. He was tried in a Jewish court for blasphemy, then in a Roman court for treason, and was finally executed as a law-breaker.

The Gospels present a mixture of legal and moral factors in their accounts of the Son's trials. They record that both the Jewish and the Romans courts followed careful legal procedures: the prisoner was arrested, charged and cross-examined; witnesses were called and questioned; the judges announced their verdicts.

But the Gospels also insist that the Son was innocent of the charges, that the witnesses lied, and that the judges' verdicts were miscarriages of justice. Furthermore, they insist that the officers of both courts were not disinterested, impartial, legal officials; but that they were flawed, sinful humans whose outer actions exposed their inner corruption.

As ever in the Gospels, the Son does not appear as a remote and distant figure. He is always deeply involved in his world, and the story of 'the Son and the cross' is the story of the Son's close interaction with the lost people whom he came to save.

The Gospels record that a series of individuals and groups of people were directly responsible for the Son's trials and death.

They report that:

- *Judas betrayed the Son to the Jewish priests for money, and handed him to them with a kiss*

- *Caiaphas and the priests arrested the Son, tried him for blasphemy, and handed him to the Roman procurator*

- *Pilate tried Jesus and passed him to the Galilean ruler*

- *Herod questioned Jesus and handed him back to Pilate*

- *Pilate then involved the crowds in the death sentence, and then handed Jesus to the Roman soldiers who crucified him*

The traitor

Matthew 10:4 ☐

Mark 3:19 ☐

Luke 6:16 ☐

Judas Iscariot is first mentioned in Matthew 10:4; Mark 3:19 and Luke 6:16. In each verse, he is numbered last of the twelve apostles and is introduced as the one who would betray Jesus.

John 6:64–71 ☐
     13:2–11 ☐
     13:27 ☐
     17:12 ☐

John's Gospel indicates that Jesus foreknew Judas would betray him, that Judas was 'doomed to destruction', and that he acted only after Satan prompted him and then possessed him. We see this in John 6:64, 71; 13:2, 11, 27; 17:12.

Acts 1:18 ☐

But this does not exonerate Judas from responsibility for the Son's death. The fact that his betrayal was foretold does not mean he was not a free agent – which is why Acts 1:18 refers to his wickedness.

John 13:25–30 ☐

Psalm 41:9. ☐

Jesus seems to regard Judas as responsible for his actions, and appears to make a final appeal to him in John 13:25–30. But Judas rejected Jesus' appeal, and so fulfilled Psalm 41:9. Jesus condemns

Judas in Mark 14:21; and Matthew 27:3–10 and Acts 1:16–20 then report that Judas condemned himself with his own hands.

Some scholars believe that Judas was a zealot who joined Jesus to liberate Israel from Rome, and betrayed him either from disillusionment or in an attempt to force his hand. Others argue, however, that John 12:3–8 and 13:29 prove Judas was morally flawed rather than politically motivated. Whatever his precise motivation, the Gospels simply state that Judas betrayed Jesus for twenty pieces of silver.

Many months earlier, in Luke 16:13, the Son had taught his disciples that it was impossible to serve God and money. When it came to the crunch, Judas chose money (as many disciples still do today) and so consigned the Son to death on the cross.

The priests

The Gospels show that the Son upset the Jewish leaders throughout his public ministry. Although it seemed to them that he posed as a Rabbi, they knew that the Son had no credentials, no training and no proper authorisation.

He feasted when he should have fasted; he mixed with disreputable people; he profaned the Sabbath by healing people; he rejected the traditions of the elders; he publicly criticised the Pharisees and called them hypocrites; and he made outrageous claims to be the lord of the Sabbath, to forgive sin, to know God uniquely as his Father, even to be equal with God. As far as the Jewish leaders were concerned, the Son was a simple blasphemer.

Caiaphas and the priests were sure that Jesus' doctrine was heretical, that his behaviour affronted the law, that he led ordinary people astray, and that he encouraged them to be disloyal to Caesar. They wanted him stopped, and were sure that they had valid political, theological and ethical reasons for silencing him. When they tried the Son, and made him testify on oath, he even made blasphemous claims for himself. It was plain to them that he deserved to die.

Despite this, Matthew 27:18 and Mark 15:10 both record Pilate's belief that the Jewish leaders were motivated by envy. They wanted him dead because he challenged their authority, while possessing an authority which they themselves lacked. When they had questioned the Son's authority in Mark 11:28, they had been silenced by his reply.

Mark 14:21 ☐

Matthew 27:3–10 ☐

Acts 1:16–20 ☐

John 12:3–8 ☐

13:29 ☐

Luke 16:13 ☐

Matthew 27:18 ☐

Mark 15:10 ☐

Mark 11:28 ☐

Matthew 2:13 ☐
        27:20 ☐

We have noted that Matthew's Gospel often highlights the issue of authority. Matthew describes two jealous plots to eliminate the Son: the first, in 2:13, by the Jewish king at the beginning of his life; the second, in 27:20, by the Jewish priests at the end of his life. Both rightly concluded that the Son was challenging their authority, and so they sought to kill him.

The procurator

Luke 23:2 ☐

The Jewish leaders passed the Son to Pontius Pilate with the words preserved in Luke 23:2 which the procurator dare not ignore. As Pilate investigated the matter, the Gospels make two strong observations.

Luke 23:4 ☐
     23:13–15 ☐
     23:22 ☐
Matthew 27:19 ☐

First, they insist that Pilate was so convinced of Jesus' innocence he declared three times that he could find no grounds for charging him. This personal conviction was confirmed to him by a message from his wife. We see this in Luke 23:4; 23:13–15; 23:22 and Matthew 27:19.

Second, the Gospels stress that Pilate wanted to avoid coming down on one side or another. He wanted to avoid sentencing Jesus because he thought he was innocent, but he also wanted to avoid exonerating him completely because he did not want to upset the Jewish leaders.

Luke 23:5–12 ☐
     23:16–22 ☐
Mark 15:6–15 ☐

The Gospels describe Pilate wriggling, as he tried to be both just and unjust at the same time. First, Luke 23:5–12 reports that he tried to transfer responsibility to Herod. When this failed, Luke 23:16–22 shows that Pilate tried to satisfy the Jews with something less than the death penalty. Next, Mark 15:6–15 describes how Pilate hoped that the crowd would select Jesus for the traditional Passover amnesty.

Matthew 27:24 ☐

Finally, when his efforts had been exhausted, Matthew 27:24 records that Pilate deviously tried to protest his innocence.

Mark 15:15 ☐
Luke 23:23–25 ☐

Yet, even before his hands were dry, Pilate handed Jesus over to die. He was a weak man, for Luke 23:20 states that Pilate wanted to release Jesus, while Mark 15:15 notes that he also wanted to satisfy the crowd. Luke 23:23–25 uses a three-fold repetition to show that the crowd won the struggle of Pilate's will: 'their' shouts prevailed; he granted 'their' demands; and, he surrendered Jesus to 'their' will.

John 19:12 ☐

Pilate knew that the Son was innocent; he knew that justice demanded his release; and John 19:12 shows that he also knew his career would flounder if justice prevailed. So Pilate silenced his conscience, compromised his beliefs, and sent the Son to the cross.

The soldiers

The soldiers who carried out Pilate's sentence were the people most immediately responsible for the Son's death. It is important to note, however, that the actual process of crucifying Jesus is not described by any Gospel; it seems that the Son's words and deeds were far more significant.

The Gospels do describe the way that the soldiers scourged and mocked the Son at the procurator's residence. First, they whipped Jesus; then, they clothed him in a purple robe, placed a 'crown' of thorns on his head and a sceptre of reed in his hand, knelt in mock homage, blindfolded him, spat on him, slapped him on the face, struck him on the head, and challenged him to identify his assailants.

Finally, according to the Roman custom, they made the Son carry his own cross to the place of execution. The weight, however, was too much, and Jesus stumbled. A man called Simon, from Cyrene in North Africa, was then pressed into carrying the cross for Jesus.

When they arrived at Golgotha, the soldiers offered Jesus some wine mixed with myrrh to dull the pain, but Jesus refused to drink it. Matthew 27:32–35; Mark 15:21–25; Luke 23:26–33 and John 19:17–18 then give no details: they do not mention a hammer and nails, nor do they refer to any pain or blood; they merely state: 'they crucified him'.

The Gospels do not suggest that the soldiers enjoyed their task or were especially cruel. They simply obeyed their orders and executed three criminals. According to Luke 23:34, 46 Jesus prayed aloud during the ordeal and made an impact on the participants: Luke 23:42–43 reports that one of the crucified criminals believed, and Luke 23:47 records that the centurion in charge of the soldiers also believed.

Matthew
27:32–35 □
Mark 15:21–25 □
Luke 23:26–33 □
John 19:17–18 □

Luke 23:34 □
23:46 □
23:42–43 □
23:47 □

THE CROSS

While the Son hung on the cross, the soldiers gambled for his clothes, some women watched from afar, and the Jewish rulers sneered that Jesus could not save himself. The Gospels report that Jesus lovingly commended his mother to John's care and John to hers, then reassured the penitent thief who was dying by his side.

At noon, darkness came to Golgotha for three hours. The Gospels do not state what happened to the Son during this time; elsewhere, however, the Scriptures reveal what occurred – we see this, for example, in Isaiah 53:5–6; Mark 10:45; 2 Corinthians 5:21; Galatians 3:13; 1 Timothy 2:5–6; Hebrews 9:28; 1 Peter 2:24 and 3:18.

The cry of forsakenness

Some people suggest that the darkness symbolised a spiritual darkness which engulfed the Son and climaxed in his cry of forsakenness. They maintain that darkness represents the idea of separation from the God who is so light that he contains no darkness.

Others suggest the opposite. They believe that God was present at the sacrifice in the form of a dark cloud, just as he had often revealed himself in a cloud at the hour of sacrifice in Old Testament times.

When the darkness ended, Jesus cried the words recorded in Mark 15:33–34. Some listeners misunderstood him, and thought that he was calling for Elijah. Although it is plain that Jesus was quoting Psalm 22:1, people still wonder what his cry meant. Some suggest that it was a cry of despair, while others consider it a cry of loneliness or victory. It is, however, a straightforward cry of genuine forsakenness.

Until the cross, though forsaken even by his closest apostles, the Son knew that his Father was with him – John 16:32 makes this clear. Now, however, he was alone, the Son was literally Father-forsaken.

On the cross, an actual separation took place between the Father and the Son: this was freely accepted by both Father and Son, and was due entirely to our sin. Jesus expressed this Father-forsakenness, by quoting the only verse in the Scriptures which accurately describes it, and which he had perfectly fulfilled.

The cries of thirst, victory and commitment

Almost immediately, the Son spoke three more phrases in quick succession.

- *I thirst*
- *It is finished*
- *Father, into your hands I commit my spirit*

His cry of thirst appears to express the toll that the Son's great spiritual sufferings had taken of him physically.

His cry of victory expressed the finality or full completion of his task. The Greek word *tetelestai* is in the perfect tense and means, 'it has been, and will be for ever, finished'. The Son had completed his redeeming rescue mission; he had accomplished what he had come into the world to do; he had borne the sins of the world; he had endured the wrath of God; he had achieved salvation for the whole world; he had given birth to new life; he had established a new covenant between God and humanity and made available the blessing of forgiveness.

His cry of commitment showed that the Son was in full control. He did not die because he was killed by sinful men; he died because he freely commended his spirit into His Father's hands.

At once, the Temple curtain (which symbolised the separation of sinners from God) was torn in two from top to bottom to demonstrate that the sin barrier had been thrown down by God, and that the way into his presence was wide open to all.

As we have seen in Part Four, thirty six hours later, the Father raised the Son from the dead and publicly vindicated him in the resurrection. This was God's decisive demonstration that the Son had not died on the cross in vain.

THE TRUTH OF THE CROSS

Everything that we consider in *Salvation by Grace* explains why Jesus attached so much importance to his death on the cross, why he instituted his memorial meal to commemorate it, and why God honoured it with a new covenant and resurrection glory.

When we fully grasp the greatness of God's eternal plan of salvation, and appreciate its foreshadowings in the Old Testament and its consummation on the last day, we can begin to understand the Son's agony of anticipation in Gethsemane, his anguish of forsakenness on the cross, and his triumphant claim to have fully accomplished our eternal salvation.

Our sin

When we start to think more deeply about the Son and the cross, we begin to glimpse three great truths of the cross. First, we start to realise just how terrible our own human sin must be, for nothing reveals the seriousness of human sin quite like the cross of Calvary.

Ultimately, the Son was not sent to the cross by Judas' greed, nor by the priests' envy, nor by Pilate's moral cowardice, but by our greed, our envy, our cowardice, and all our other sins – and by his loving determination to bear their judgement and so to remove them completely. It surely is not possible for us to look at the drama of the cross without feeling real shame at our personal complicity.

If there really was no way by which the holy God could righteously have forgiven our sin except by bearing it himself, in the Son, on the cross, then our sin must be extremely serious indeed. Once people have begun to grasp this truth they are ready to trust the Son as the Saviour whom they so desperately need.

His love

Second, the cross reveals that God's love must be so great as to be almost beyond human comprehension. We consider this 'revelatory' aspect of the cross in *Salvation by Grace*.

The Father could have abandoned humanity to its fate. He could have left us to reap the fruit of our sin and to perish in our wickedness. After all, this is what we deserve and it is often what we want. But God did not act like this. Because he loves us, he came after us in Christ. He pursued us to the anguish of the cross – where he lovingly bore our sin, our guilt, our judgement and our death. It surely is not possible to look at the motivating love of the cross and to remain unmoved.

When people start to appreciate this truth, they are eager to love the Son as the Lord whom they need so much.

Free grace

Third, the cross declares that salvation must be a free gift. As the Son purchased it fully with his blood, there can be nothing left for us to pay. And as he claimed that his task was 'finished' on the cross, there can be nothing left for us to contribute. It is all God; it is all all-grace.

PART NINE

the return of the son

The Gospels make it clear that the cross is not the end of the Son's story. We have seen in Part Four that he rose from the dead, ascended to heaven, sat down at the Father's right hand, poured out the Spirit as he had promised, gave gifts to the church, and began the heavenly work of intercession which continues to this day.

But even all this is not the end of the Son's story, for the whole Bible looks forward to the Son's return to earth at the end of time. This is not a tiny truth which is tucked away in a half-verse here and there, it is a major thread of hope which runs through the whole Scriptures.

THE HOPE OF THE OLD TESTAMENT

As we have stressed throughout this *Sword of the Spirit* series, the biblical saga of hope and covenant promise began when God called Abram to leave his family home. What started as the purposeful journey of a small group of nomads became a pilgrimage through history of a people packed with divine hope.

Genesis 12:1–3 ☐

All biblical hope is based on God's covenant promise in Genesis 12:1–3. God guaranteed to provide Abram and his descendants with:

- *a land*

- *a great nation*

- *a blessing*

Genesis 17:7 ☐

This three-fold promise was repeated and extended many times down the ages, but it is always summarised in the phrase which is first mentioned in Genesis 17:7. This covenant relationship sums up the whole purpose of God for humanity.

Throughout the Old Testament, Abraham's descendants looked back to these covenant promises and claimed them as their destiny. When they were weak, enslaved and exiled, the promises enabled them to sustain their national identity and to believe that God had a future and a hope for them. And when they were strong and prosperous, the promises helped them to maintain a forward view and a future attitude.

The children of Abraham knew that *Yahweh* was a God of promise, and this knowledge helped them to recognise that the present situation was never God's final act, and to fix their hopes on the future, on God's complete fulfilment of his promise to Abraham.

The hope of the prophets

As we see in *Ministry in the Spirit*, it was part of the prophets' calling to declare God's intentions about the future. Most of the prophets whose books are included in the Old Testament ministered when Israel had begun to focus too much on the past. People were looking back to the exodus from Egypt, to David's reign, to the first temple, and so on.

Amos 2:6 ☐
     5:18 ☐
     5:23 ☐

Almost eight hundred years before Christ, Amos proclaimed that the most important event for God's people lay in the future, not in the past. He called it 'the day of the Lord' – we see this in Amos 5:18–20 – and he declared that it would be a day of darkness not light.

Isaiah 30:1–2 ☐
     30:15–17 ☐

Jeremiah 5:1 ☐
     7:4–7 ☐

At a time of national prosperity, Amos announced catastrophe – we see this in Amos 2:6; 5:18; 5:23. Other prophets preached much the same message, for example, Isaiah 30:1–2, 15–17; Jeremiah 5:1; 7:4–7.

Through these and many other passages, the prophets mocked Jewish attempts to find security and hope in anything other than God himself. They persistently announced God's opposition to all human attempts to find security in anything less than himself and his will.

Yet, despite the severity of the judgements that they announced, the prophets never pretended that these would be God's last acts. They also proclaimed a message of future promise, which they based on:

- *God's burning love* – Hosea 11:8–9; Lamentations 3:21–24

- *God's faithfulness to his covenant promise* – Isaiah 37:35

- *God's concern for his honour* – Ezekiel 36:22–23; Isaiah 48:11

- *God's essential creativity* – Isaiah 43:1; 49:6

Although the prophets declared that the day of the Lord would be a day of darkness, they also proclaimed that God's original promise to Abraham still stood. They insisted that God would completely fulfil it.

The prophets looked forward and announced that there would be:

- *a new David* – 2 Samuel 7:12–16; Isaiah 9:6–7; 11:1–9; Jeremiah 33:15–16; Zechariah 9:9

- *a new Jerusalem* – Isaiah 2:2–4; 65:17–25; Jeremiah 33:16; Zechariah 14:11, 16

- *a new prosperity* – Isaiah 65:21; Ezekiel 47:12; Joel 3:18; Amos 9:13–15; Micah 4:4

- *a new temple* – Ezekiel 40–48

- *a new Israel* – Jeremiah 30:8–9; Amos 9:11–15; Micah 4:6–7; Hosea 3:5; Zephaniah 3:20

- *a new relationship with God* – Hosea 2:14–16, 19

- *a new covenant* – Jeremiah 31:31–34

- *a new heart* – Ezekiel 18:30–32; 36:25–28

- *a new exodus* – Isaiah 40:1–11; 43:18–19; 52:12; Ezekiel 20:33–34; Hosea 2:14–15

- *a new heaven and new earth* – Isaiah 65:17–22

The prophets could make these announcements because they knew that God acted and controlled history. They discerned his purposeful

Hosea 11:8–9 ☐
Lamentations 3:21–24 ☐
Isaiah 37:35 ☐
Ezekiel 36:22–23 ☐
Isaiah 48:11 ☐
43:1 ☐
49:6 ☐

2 Samuel 7:12–16 ☐
Isaiah 9:6–7 ☐
11:1–9 ☐
Jeremiah 33:15–16 ☐
Zechariah 9:9 ☐
Isaiah 2:2–4 ☐
65:17–25 ☐
Jeremiah 33:16 ☐
Zechariah 14:11 ☐
14:16 ☐
Isaiah 65:21 ☐
Ezekiel 47:12 ☐
Joel 3:18 ☐
Amos 9:13–15 ☐
Micah 4:4 ☐
Ezekiel 40–48 ☐
Jeremiah 30:8–9 ☐
Amos 9:11–15 ☐
Micah 4:6–7 ☐
Hosea 3:5 ☐
Zephaniah 3:20 ☐
Hosea 2:14–16 ☐
2:19 ☐
Jeremiah 31:31–34 ☐
Ezekiel 18:30–32 ☐
36:25–28 ☐
Isaiah 40:1–11 ☐
43:18–19 ☐
52:12 ☐
Ezekiel 20:33–34 ☐
Hosea 2:14–15 ☐
Isaiah 65:17–22 ☐

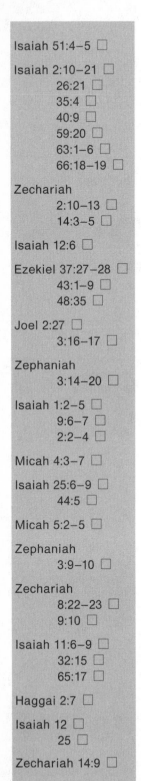

Isaiah 51:4–5 ☐

Isaiah 2:10–21 ☐
26:21 ☐
35:4 ☐
40:9 ☐
59:20 ☐
63:1–6 ☐
66:18–19 ☐

Zechariah
2:10–13 ☐
14:3–5 ☐

Isaiah 12:6 ☐

Ezekiel 37:27–28 ☐
43:1–9 ☐
48:35 ☐

Joel 2:27 ☐
3:16–17 ☐

Zephaniah
3:14–20 ☐

Isaiah 1:2–5 ☐
9:6–7 ☐
2:2–4 ☐

Micah 4:3–7 ☐

Isaiah 25:6–9 ☐
44:5 ☐

Micah 5:2–5 ☐

Zephaniah
3:9–10 ☐

Zechariah
8:22–23 ☐
9:10 ☐

Isaiah 11:6–9 ☐
32:15 ☐
65:17 ☐

Haggai 2:7 ☐

Isaiah 12 ☐
25 ☐

Zechariah 14:9 ☐

activity in past and present events, and were sure that he would carry on acting in similar ways. They looked to God to direct the course of history, to do something about the state of his people, and to intervene among other nations – we see this, for example, in Isaiah 51:4–5.

The prophets were also sure that there would be both a continuity and a discontinuity between God's actions in the past and the future. They announced that he would do surprising things and bring his people blessing and security beyond their imagination: their constant repetition of the word 'new' underlines this sense of discontinuity. But their use of words like 'covenant' and 'exodus' demonstrates that they were also aware of a real sense of continuity with the past.

They promised that, although God would do new things, his purpose for the world would be consistent with his acts in the past; that, although he would reveal himself in the future in the ultimate salvation of humanity, he was already revealing himself within Israel's history.

The prophetic hope can be summarised in three common expressions:

- *God will come* – Isaiah 2:10–21; 26:21; 35:4; 40:9; 59:20; 63:1–6; 66:18–19; Zechariah 2:10–13; 14:3–5

- *God will be with his people* – Isaiah 12:6; Ezekiel 37:27–28; 43:1–9; 48:35; Joel 2:27; 3:16–17; Zephaniah 3:14–20

- *God will rule –*
  with justice and integrity – Isaiah 1:2–5; 9:7
  with peace – Isaiah 2:2–4; 9:6; Micah 4:3–4
  permanently – Isaiah 9:7; Micah 4:6–7
  universally – Isaiah 25:6–9; 44:5; Micah 5:2–5; Zephaniah 3:9–10; Zechariah 8:22–23; 9:10
  on earth – Isaiah 11:6–9; 32:15; 65:17; Haggai 2:7
  in worship and rejoicing – Isaiah 12; 25; Zechariah 14:9

The Old Testament never declares when these events will occur, because it never distinguished between the immediate and the ultimate fulfilment of prophecy (we consider this in *Ministry in the Spirit*). Instead, it focuses attention on the God who keeps his promises rather than on any chronology of the future.

This basic summary of Old Testament hope is an important foundation for an accurate understanding of the great hope of the Son which is unveiled in the New Testament.

THE HOPE OF THE SON

In 2 Corinthians 1:20, the apostle Paul makes the staggering claim that Jesus is God's 'Yes' to all God's promises, that he is the one in whom all the Old Testament prophetic hopes and covenant promises are fulfilled. If we do not know those hopes, we will not appreciate the enormity of Paul's words.

We have seen in Part Five (and, especially, in The Rule of God) that Jesus proclaimed the kingdom of God – that he announced the arrival of the rule of God. This was the central theme of all his teaching.

The Son declared in words that God's long-promised rule had begun; he demonstrated in deeds that a new experience of God's saving power had come; and he displayed his anointing with the Spirit as a key evidence of the kingdom's presence.

Jesus stressed that the kingdom of God was especially for the hurting, and he revealed that:

- the King of the kingdom is a Father – Matthew 6:9–10; Luke 12:32

- the character of the kingdom is forgiveness – Matthew 18:23–35; Mark 2:10, 15–17; Luke 7:36–50; 15; 18:9–14

- the purpose of the kingdom is a new order – Matthew 11:25–26; 18:3; 22:1–10; Mark 10:14; Luke 1:51–53; 6:20–25; 13:30; 16:19–31

- the demands of the kingdom are repentance and trust – Matthew 5:25–26; 6:24–34; 23:5–12; Mark 1:15; 8:34–35; 10:17–31; Luke 6:27–36; 13:2–3; 14:26; 15:11–32

Now and not yet

We have also seen that, although God's rule had come in Christ, it had not yet fully come. The kingdom was present in the sense that the blessings of the new age were already being experienced through the Son's ministry. But its full realisation (in the sense of God's total triumph over evil and his establishment of a universal realm of permanent justice, peace and worship) still remained an object of hope for the future.

Matthew 6:10 ☐

Luke 13:29 ☐

Matthew 13:33 ☐

Mark 4:26–32 ☐

Luke 12:32 ☐

Mark 8:31 ☐
        9:31 ☐
        10:33–34 ☐
        10:38 ☐

Luke 12:50 ☐

The kingdom was present, yet it was hidden; a new power had been unleashed, yet many failed to recognise it. Nevertheless, a day would come when doubt, opposition and hiddenness would give way to the full realisation of God's rule. So Jesus taught his disciples to pray the prayer of Matthew 6:10 and to believe the promise of Luke 13:29.

When Jesus spoke about the coming kingdom, about his kingdom hope for the future, he emphasised three points:

- *the kingdom will progressively grow* – Matthew 13:33; Mark 4:26–32

- *the kingdom will come through grace* – Luke 12:32

- *the kingdom will come through his own suffering and death* – Mark 8:31; 9:31; 10:33–34; 10:38; Luke 12:50

The vindication of the Son

The Gospels make it plain that Jesus expected not only to die, but also to be vindicated by God. The Son knew he was destined to suffer, and that God's public approval of his work was beyond his suffering.

Mark 9:31 ☐

Matthew 10:23 ☐
        24:44 ☐
        25:31 ☐

Mark 8:38 ☐
        13:26 ☐
        14:62 ☐

Luke 18:8 ☐

Mark 8:38 ☐
        13:26–27 ☐

Matthew
        25:31–46 ☐

Luke 21:36 ☐

Sometimes Jesus spoke about this vindication in terms of resurrection, as in Mark 9:31; but at other times he expressed it in terms of the Son's return to earth in the future – for example, Matthew 10:23; 24:44; 25:31; Mark 8:38; 13:26; 14:62; Luke 18:8.

The Son's words about vindication always assume that the one who comes in glory will be the same one who was raised from the dead after three days. We see this, for example, in Mark 14:62.

Although Jesus announces his resurrection and his return in similar ways, he always distinguishes between the outcomes of these two events. Whenever he speaks about the Son's coming, he associates it with the final judgement of humanity and with the full establishment of God's kingdom – as in Mark 8:38; 13:26–27; Matthew 25:31–46 and Luke 21:36. But Jesus always speaks about his resurrection in terms of it being his *personal* vindication – rather than the ultimate vindication of all God's purposes.

This shows that the Son expected to die, to be vindicated by the Father through resurrection from death, and ultimately to come again to bring God's purposes for the world to their complete fulfilment.

The hope of the Son

Just as the prophets were more concerned with *God's* actions in the future than with an exact chronology of the future, so the Son teaches much about what God will do and little about when he will do it. The Gospels report that Jesus' prophetic hope contained several distinctive elements.

- *He foresaw catastrophe for the Jewish nation* – Mark 13:2 and Luke 19:42–44.

- *He envisaged a day when people from other nations would be part of the kingdom; and he expected that his followers, the church, would fulfil the role of God's people* – Matthew 8:11–12 and 16:18.

- *He anticipated a conflict between his followers and the forces opposed to them* – Mark 13.

- *He declared that his followers would be vindicated: they would find that God would accept them and show that their decision to follow Jesus had been correct* – Matthew 10:32; Mark 8:35; Luke 6:22–23; 12:32.

- *He announced that he would return in triumph to complete God's purposes* – Mark 13:24–27.

THE PURPOSE OF THE SON'S RETURN

Although the Son's prophetic descriptions of the mode and time of his coming are deliberately vague, he makes the purpose of his coming startlingly clear. He proves from the Scriptures that there will be resurrected life, and then promises that he will come again to raise his people to the new life of the kingdom and to gather them into his presence from all over the world – Mark 12:18–27 and 13:26–27.

The Son also promises that he will return to judge the lives of all people, and that this will divide those who have entered God's kingdom from those who have chosen to remain outside – Matthew 24:40–41 and Mark 9:33–48.

Mark 13:2 ☐

Luke 19:42–44 ☐

Matthew 8:11–12 ☐
16:18 ☐

Mark 13 ☐

Matthew 10:32 ☐

Mark 8:35 ☐

Luke 6:22–23 ☐
12:32 ☐

Mark 13:24–27 ☐

Mark 12:18–27 ☐
13:26–27 ☐

Matthew
24:40–41 ☐

Mark 9:33–48 ☐

Matthew 25:41 ☐

The Son also promises that he will come again to destroy Satan and all his works completely – Matthew 25:41.

Mark 13:31 ☐

Mark 12:25 ☐

And the Son promises that the world will be renewed and that God's people will enter his final and perfect kingdom – Mark 13:31. Jesus never provides a detailed description of this eternal existence; but, in Mark 12:25, he clearly denies that it will simply be a continuation of present earthly existence at a higher level.

Matthew 25:10 ☐
25:21–23 ☐

Luke 6:21–23 ☐

Matthew 5:8 ☐
25:1–13 ☐

Instead of offering titillating details, Jesus gave a series of imaginative pictures to inspire our faith. He promises that God's people will enter into joy in his presence, and suggests this is like the joy of a wedding celebration – Matthew 25:10, 21–23. There will be laughter and dancing; the hungry will be filled – Luke 6:21–23; the pure will see God – Matthew 5:8; and he himself, the bridegroom, will be the centre of attention – Matthew 25:1–13.

Mark 14:58 ☐

Luke 16:9 ☐

He promises that the community of his people will be together at worship – Mark 14:58 – and that their joyful excitement will be like pilgrims who have reached their destination after a testing journey. This is implied in Luke 16:9, where Jesus speaks of 'eternal tents' – the fulfilment of the ever-moving tabernacle in the wilderness.

Matthew 8:11 ☐
25:34 ☐

And he promises that this new community will bring Jews and Gentiles together in one united fellowship – Matthew 8:11 and 25:34.

THE RESULTS OF THE SON'S RETURN

The New Testament makes it clear that the return of the Son will complete God's work of rescuing humanity. On that day, the Son will be visibly revealed to all humanity in total triumph and great glory. He may have come for the first time in obscurity and weakness, but his return will be an unmistakable event which is public, triumphant, glorious and universal.

The Son's apparent absence from earth will give way to his impressive presence on earth. His mysterious hiddenness will be replaced by an open manifestation of his perfect character and divine splendour. When the Son finally returns, there simply will be no room for doubt about who he is and whether he has really come or not.

The Son's return will result not only in the unveiling of all that is hidden about Christ, but also in the unveiling of all that is hidden about humanity. The New Testament stresses that God's judgement of individual men and women is one of the main reasons for the Son's return – we see this, for example, in 1 Corinthians 4:5 and 15:45. On the last day, all the ultimate issues of life will be exposed; and all our excuses and ambiguities will vanish.

1 Corinthians 15:24–25 and Revelation 20:7–15 show that the Son's return will also result in total conquest of all that is evil. His coming will mean the removal of suffering, the end of every evil thought and action, the vindication of those who have suffered for righteousness' sake, and the unmasking of every oppressor. Satan and his hosts will finally be dealt with – for all eternity.

When the Son comes, he will gather his people together into his presence and bring resurrection to those who have died before his coming. But the Son will not only change believers in his resurrection power, he will also transform the whole universe. As we see in *Knowing the Father*, God's purposes are much bigger than just the personal destiny of individual people. 2 Peter 3:13 underlines the truth that God is going to bring about a whole new order where righteousness will be at home.

Finally, the Son's return will result in the end and completion of all history. The Bible does not present the course of history as circular or aimless or everlasting. Instead, it presents history as a movement towards a goal, as a journey towards the perfect kingdom of God; it presents God as always acting in history to accomplish and fulfil his purposes.

At the great climax of history, God will act through the return of his Son to end all opposition to him and his will, and to establish his eternal kingdom. This dynamic divine intervention will complete what the Son has accomplished on the cross and has achieved through his body, the church.

Our certain hope

This, then, is the great hope of the Son, that the God whose rule was already at work in his earthly ministry will bring his plan to completion in his coming again in glory. At his return, all the Old Testament pictures of a permanent kingdom of justice, peace and

1 Corinthians 4:5 ☐
15:45 ☐

1 Corinthians
15:24–25 ☐
Revelation
20:7–15 ☐

2 Peter 3:13 ☐

Matthew 6:33 ☐

Mark 10:16–31 ☐

Luke 11:2 ☐

worship (which are prophetically anticipated in the Son's ministry and his people's lives) will reach the glory of complete fulfilment.

Until that time, however, Matthew 6:33; Mark 10:16–31 and Luke 11:2 show that the Son continues to present us with the challenge of making sure that the kingdom has first place in our lives, of giving up everything for the kingdom, and of praying continually for its coming.

We can do all these with total confidence, because we know that the promise-keeping Father will keep his word to us, will complete what he has begun in our lives, will make his home among us, and will ensure that the Son reigns over all for ever and ever.

ACTIVITIES for individuals and small groups

the fully human son

How do the Gospels of Matthew, Mark and Luke show that Jesus is a first-century human?

....

....

....

....

How does the Gospel of John show that Jesus is fully human?

....

....

....

How do the Gospels make it plain that Jesus was quite different from all other humans?

....

....

What do these passages teach about Jesus' historicity and humanity? Romans 1:3; 5:12–21; 9:5; 1 Corinthians 11:23–26; 15:4, 21–22; 2 Corinthians 5:21; 8:9; 10:1; Galatians 1:19; 4:4; Philippians 2:6–8; 2 Thessalonians 3:5; 1 Timothy 2:5.

....

....

....

....

How do the Gospels suggest that Jesus is sinless?

....

....

....

Why was it so important for Jesus to be sinless?

....

....

THE CHRIST

What does the title 'the Christ' mean? What does it teach you about Jesus?

....

....

....

....

....

What does the story of Cyrus (in Isaiah 41:25; 45:1–13; 47) reveal about the Christ?

....

....

....

How do Israel's Old Testament kings, priests and prophets point to the Christ?

....

....

....

Why didn't the Jewish people recognise that Jesus was the Christ?

....

....

Why did the first believers stress to Jews that Jesus was descended from king David?

....

....

Jesus' followers are known as 'Christians'. What does it mean to you to be a 'Christian'?

....

....

....

....

....

THE SON OF MAN

What do these passages teach you about the Son of Man?

Mark 2:10, 28; John 9:35–39 ....

....

Matthew 8:20; 11:19 ....

....

Matthew 12:32 ....

....

Matthew 13:37; John 6:27 ....

....

Mark 8:31; 12:23–24 ....

....

Mark 10:45; John 3:13–14 ....

....

Mark 14:21, 41 ....

....

Mark 8:38; 13:26; 14:62 ....

....

Matthew 13:41; Luke 12:8 ....

....

Matthew 19:28; Luke 21:36 ....

....

When you take an overview of these passages, which three aspects of Jesus' character come across most clearly?

....

....

....

the fully divine son

John's Gospel begins with a 'genealogy' which makes it clear that the fully human Jesus is also the eternal Word, the full revelation of the fully divine God.

What do these passages teach you about Jesus' nature and activities as the Word?

Genesis 1; Psalm 33:6–9; 147:15–18; 148:8 ....

....

Psalm 147:15; Isaiah 55:11; Hosea 6:5 ....

....

Psalm 119:9, 105; Jeremiah 20:9; Ezekiel 33:7 ....

....

Job 28:12–27; Proverbs 8:1–9, 12 ....

....

John 1:1–18 is the clearest biblical description of 'the Word'. What does it suggest to you about Jesus' relation with:

The Father ....

....

The world ....

....

Human beings ....

....

Why are Jesus' 'I am' sayings so important?

....

....

What do they reveal to you about Jesus?

....

....

....

THE LORD

What did the title 'the Lord' mean to Jews of Jesus' day?

....

....

When was Jesus recognised as 'the Lord'?

....

....

How do the different gospels draw attention to Jesus' divine status as 'the Lord'?

....

....

....

What does it mean to you to know and follow Jesus as Lord?

....

....

....

The first sermon of the Church Age climaxed, in Acts 2:36, with the declaration that 'God has made this Jesus, whom you crucified, both Lord and Christ'.

Why is it important to proclaim Jesus as both Lord and Christ?

....

....

....

How can you explain Jesus 'Lordship' and 'Christhood' to modern unbelievers in contemporary terms that they can understand?

....

....

....

....

THE SON OF GOD

What do these passages suggest to you about Jesus' divine sonship?
Matthew 11:25–30; Mark 1:11; 9:2–7; 12:1–12, 35–37; 13:32; Luke 10:21–24 and 22:29

....

....

....

....

John's Gospel reveals Jesus particularly clearly as 'the Son of God'. What do these passages from John teach you about the Son's relationship with the Father?

3:34; 5:36–38; 7:29; 11:42; 17:4–5 ....

....

3:35; 5:20; 10:17; 17:23–24 ....

....

5:19, 30; 14:28–31; 15:10 ....

....

5:19–23; 10:30; 14:11, 20; 17:11 ....

....

11:41; 12:28; 17:1, 5, 11, 21, 24, 25 ....

....

6:46; 8:19; 10:15; 14:8–9 ....

....

10:18; 12:49–50; 14:24; 15:15; 16:25 ....

....

8:16; 13:3; 16:15; 18:11 ....

....

14:12, 28; 16:10, 16, 28; 20:17 ....

....

a unique being

How does the Gospel of Matthew mainly present Jesus?

....

....

What does Matthew highlight and emphasise?

....

....

....

Which of Matthew's unique insights impressed you the most?

....

....

How does the Gospel of Mark mainly present Jesus?

....

....

What does Mark highlight and emphasise?

....

....

....

Which of Mark's unique insights impressed you the most?

....

....

How does the Gospel of Luke mainly present Jesus?

....

....

What does Luke highlight and emphasise?

....

....

Which of Luke's unique insights impressed you the most?

....

....

How does the Gospel of John mainly present Jesus?

....

....

What does John highlight and emphasise?

....

....

....

Which of John's unique insights impressed you the most?

....

....

Why do the four Gospels handle Jesus' birth so differently? What does this mean for the way we celebrate Christmas?

....

....

....

....

Which Gospel presents the side of Jesus that you feel you know least well?

....

What changes do you need to makes to ensure that you know, and that you proclaim, every side of Jesus' nature and character?

....

....

....

....

....

....

THE FOUR HYMNS

What does Philippians 2:5–11 teach you about the Son's:

pre-existence ....

....

incarnation ....

....

exaltation ....

....

What impression does this hymn create of Jesus?

....

....

....

If you had to highlight the key aspects of Jesus' nature, what would they be?

....

....

....

What does Colossians 1:15–20 teach you about the Son's:

supremacy ....

....

sustenance ....

....

fullness ....

....

What do 1 Timothy 3:16 and Hebrews 1:3 suggest to you about the Son?

....

....

....

a unique life

According to the Gospel of Luke, what is unusual about Jesus' nativity?

....

....

....

....

According to the Gospel of Matthew, what is unusual about Jesus' nativity?

....

....

....

....

How do these two Gospels underline the fact that Jesus was born of a virgin?

....

....

....

....

What clues do Mark and John contain to the virgin birth?

....

....

....

....

What does the virgin birth mean to you? Why is it important?

....

....

....

....

....

THE RESURRECTION

What are the key evidences for the resurrection?

....

....

....

....

How can you effectively challenge those who do not believe in the resurrection?

....

....

....

....

How did Jesus predict his resurrection?

....

....

....

How does the Bible report the resurrection?

....

....

....

How does Paul proclaim the resurrection in 1 Corinthians 15:3–11?

....

....

....

What does the resurrection mean to you?

....

....

....

THE ASCENSION

Jesus' birth and resurrection are central events in most modern churches, but his ascension is often overlooked. Why do some churches pay the ascension so little attention?

....

....

....

....

How does the New Testament describe the ascension?

....

....

....

What do these passages suggest about the significance of the ascension?
John 7:39; Acts 2:14–36; 3:21; 5:31; Romans 10:6–7; Ephesians 1:20; 4:8–10; Colossians 3:1;
1 Thessalonians 1:10; 2 Thessalonians 1:7; Philippians 2:9–11; 3:20; 1 Timothy 3:16; Hebrews
1:3; 4:14; 5:6; 6:20; 7:15–17, 21, 26; 8:1; 9:24; 10:12; 12:2

....

....

....

....

....

....

....

What does the ascension mean to you? How should we celebrate it in the church today?

....

....

....

....

....

a unique mission

What are the main sides of Jesus' mission? Which side does each Gospel most emphasise?

....

....

....

....

How can we see these sides in Jesus' baptism?

....

....

....

....

What is the prophetic sequence of events in Jesus' baptism?

....

....

How can we see this sequence in all of Jesus' mission?

....

....

....

....

Which elements of Jesus' baptism do you stress most? Why is this?

....

....

....

Which element do you stress least? Why is this?

....

....

....

What could the different elements of the baptism symbolise about Jesus' whole mission?

....

....

....

....

How can you develop a more fully-rounded approach to mission and discipleship?

....

....

....

....

THE SON'S MISSION STATEMENT

What does Luke 4:18–19 teach you about Jesus' mission?

....

....

....

....

What does Luke 7:18–22 teach you about Jesus' mission?

....

....

....

....

What does Mark 1:21–34 teach you about Jesus' mission?

....

....

....

....

HE BREAKS THE POWER OF EVIL

How did Satan attack Jesus during his life?

....

....

....

How did Jesus attack Satan during his life?

....

....

....

What prompted Jesus to break the grip of evil in a particular person's life?

....

....

....

How, practically, did Jesus release people from the grip of evil?

....

....

....

What impact did this have on the people of Jesus' day?

....

....

....

What is your experience of this aspect of Jesus' mission?

....

....

....

....

....

HE HEALS THE SICK

What are some of the different ways that we can think of the Son's healing mission?

....

....

....

How central was healing to Jesus' mission?

....

....

How central is healing to your mission in the world?

....

....

What prompted Jesus to heal a particular person?

....

....

....

How, practically, did Jesus minister healing?

....

....

....

What impact did this have on people?

....

....

What is your experience of this aspect of Jesus' mission?

....

....

....

....

HE PROCLAIMS THE KINGDOM

What did Jesus teach about the kingdom?

....

....

....

....

What do Jesus' parables teach about the kingdom?

....

....

....

....

What do Mark 1:15–20 and Matthew 4:17–22 teach about the way Jesus proclaimed the kingdom?

....

....

....

....

What was the ultimate purpose of Jesus' unique mission?

....

....

....

....

What is God saying to you about your share in Jesus' mission?

....

....

....

....

the son and the spirit

What are Mark's two great claims in Mark 1:1–15? Why are these so significant?

....
....
....
....

How does each Gospel underline the fact that Jesus uniquely bears the Holy Spirit?

....
....
....
....

Why does John the Baptist stress Jesus' ministry of baptising people with the Holy Spirit?

....
....
....

THE SON REVEALS THE SPIRIT

How could Jesus reveal the Spirit?

....
....

What do these passages teach about the link between the Son and the Spirit?

John 3:16; 5:43; 16:28 ....

....

John 5:43; 14:26 ....

....

John 14:16–18 ....

....

John 14:6, 17; 15:26; 16:13 ....

....

John 8:28; 12:28; 16:14; 17:4 ....

....

John 8:14; 15:26–27 ....

....

John 15:26–27 ....

....

John 16:8–11 ....

....

John 1:10–11, 14:17 ....

....

John 7:7; 16:8 ....

....

THE SPIRIT OF SONSHIP

What set Jesus apart as the messianic Son of God, and brought forth the voice from heaven at his baptism which declared his sonship?

....

....

What does Romans 8:14–17 teach you about the relationship between the Spirit and sonship?

....

....

....

....

THE SPIRIT OF SERVANTHOOD

What is the significance of the Spirit coming upon Jesus 'like a dove' at his baptism?

....

....

....

....

What do these passages teach about the relationship between the Spirit and suffering service?

Acts 4:29–31 ....

....

Acts 20:22–23 ....

....

1 Peter 4:13–16 ....

....

What difference is the Spirit making to the way that you serve God and other people?

....

....

....

....

In what different ways does the New Testament show the Spirit enabling disciples to witness?

....

....

....

What difference is the Spirit making to the way that you witness?

....

....

....

....

the son and the father

How, essentially, did Jesus know that he was the Son?

....

....

....

What did the Father's words at the Son's baptism in the Jordan reveal – from the Old Testament – about Jesus' sonship?

....

....

....

How, in the wilderness, did the devil attack Jesus' consciousness of his sonship? And how did Jesus defeat the temptation?

....

....

....

....

How does the devil attack your awareness of your sonship, and how do you deal with this temptation?

....

....

....

....

How does Jesus' relationship with the Father enable him to face his passion?

....

....

....

....

How does your relationship with the Father enable you to handle hardship?

....

....

....

....

THE SON DEPENDS ON THE FATHER

In what ways does the Father depend on the Son?

....

....

....

In what ways do you depend on the Son?

....

....

....

In what ways does the Son depend on the Father?

....

....

....

In what ways do you depend on the Father?

....

....

....

What is God saying to you about depending on him?

....

....

....

What do these verses teach you about the Son's submission to the Father?

Hebrews 10:7 ....

....

John 6:38 ....

....

Luke 7:8 ....

....

John 5:19–20 ....

....

1 Corinthians 15:28 ....

....

Philippians 2:10 ....

....

What do these verses say to you about the way you submit to the Father?

....

....

....

....

How does the Son listen to the Father?

....

....

....

....

How do you listen to the Father?

....

....

....

....

the son and the cross

What do the different events of the last supper teach you about the cross?

....
....
....
....

What does the communion service mean to you?

....
....
....
....

GETHSEMANE

Why did Jesus seem to flinch from God's will in the garden?

....
....
....

What enabled him willingly to accept the Father's will?

....
....
....

With which aspect of God's will for your life do you most struggle?

....
....
....
....

THE TRIALS

Why did Judas betray Jesus?

....

....

....

Why did the priests press for Jesus to be killed?

....

....

....

Why did Pilate condemn Jesus to death?

....

....

....

Why did the soldiers nail Jesus to the cross?

....

....

....

What is the weakness which most causes you to let Jesus down? What is God saying to you about this?

....

....

....

....

Why do the Gospels not describe Jesus' physical ordeal on the cross?

....

....

....

THE CROSS

What do these passages reveal about the cross?
Isaiah 53:5–6; Mark 10:45; 2 Corinthians 5:21; Galatians 3:13; 1 Timothy 2:5–6; Hebrews 9:28; 1 Peter 2:24 and 3:18

....

....

....

....

What do Jesus' words on the cross to Mary, John and the thief reveal about the Son?

....

....

....

....

What does Jesus' cry of forsakenness mean to you?

....

....

....

....

Why was Jesus' thirsty, and why did he refuse the drink?

....

....

....

What had Jesus finished?

....

....

....

....

the return of the son

What do these passages teach you about the way that God will act in the future?
Isaiah 37:35; 43:1; 48:11; 49:6; Lamentations 3:21–24; Ezekiel 36:22–23; Hosea 11:8–9

....

....

What did the prophets announce that there would be?

....

....

....

Which of these promises have been fulfilled in Christ, and which still await fulfilment?

....

....

....

....

What do these sets of passages teach about the prophetic hope of the Old Testament?
Isaiah 2:10–21; 26:21; 35:4; 40:9; 59:20; 63:1–6; 66:18–19; Zechariah 2:10–13; 14:3–5

....

Isaiah 12:6; Ezekiel 37:27–28; 43:1–9; 48:35; Joel 2:27; 3:16–17; Zephaniah 3:14–20

....

Isaiah 1:2–5; 2:2–4; 9:6–7; 11:6–9; 25:6–9; 32:15; 44:5; 65:17; Micah 4:3–7; 5:2–5; Haggai 2:7; Zephaniah 3:9–10; Zechariah 8:22–23; 9:10; 14:9

....

....

THE HOPE OF THE SON

What does 2 Corinthians 1:20 reveal to you about the relationship between Jesus and the hope and promises of the Old Testament?

....

....

What, practically, does this mean to you?

....

....

In these passages, what did Jesus promise about the future?

Mark 13:2 and Luke 19:42–44 ....

....

....

Matthew 8:11–12 and 16:18 ....

....

....

Mark 13 ....

....

....

Matthew 10:32; Mark 8:35; Luke 6:22–23; 12:32 ....

....

....

Mark 13:24–27 ....

....

....

Why did Jesus say nothing about 'when' these events will take place?

....

....

THE PURPOSE OF THE SON'S RETURN

What do these passages promise about what will happen when the Son returns?

Mark 12:18–27; 13:26–27 ....

....

Matthew 24:40–41; Mark 9:33–48 ....

....

Matthew 25:41 ....

....

Mark 13:31 ....

....

Matthew 5:8; 25:1–13, 21–23; Luke 6:21–23 ....

....

Mark 14:58 ....

....

Matthew 8:11; 25:34 ....

....

What are you most looking forward to about the Son's return?

....

....

....

What is the most important truth that you have learnt about the Son?

....

....

What is God calling you to do, or change, as a result of working through this book?

....

....

....

....